Soldiers
with
Little Feet

Teaching Our Children to
Express Compassionate Love

DIAN LAYTON

Destiny Image® Publishers, Inc.
P.O. Box 310
Shippensburg, PA 17257-0351

"Speaking to the Purposes of God
for this Generation"

ISBN 0-914903-86-1

For Worldwide Distribution
Printed in the U.S.A.

Seventh Printing: 2002   Eighth Printing: 2003

This book and all other Destiny Image, Revival Press, MercyPlace, Fresh Bread, and Destiny Image Fiction books are available at Christian bookstores and distributors worldwide:

For a U.S. bookstore nearest you, call **1-800-722-6774**.
For more information on foreign distributors,
call **1-800-722-6774**.
Or reach us on the Internet:

www.destinyimage.com

I dedicate these pages to

my husband Barry, who has continually believed
in me and lovingly commanded me to do God's will
— "Get writing that book!"

Soldiers With Little Feet

I hear the sound of an army
Of soldiers with little feet;
And they are marching into battle
In the Name of the King of kings!

Oh, Lord, fill them up with Your power,
With Your wisdom, and with Your love.
Oh, Lord, raise them up in this hour —
Little people who **know** their God, oh yeah,
Little people who **know** their God!

...Because the people who **know** their God shall
have mega-muscles and go on *ADVENTURES!*
(Dan. 11:32b, Hugga-Wugga Version)

Introduction

Picture yourself living around the year 0 A.D. (give or take a few years). For those who believe, there is a sense of excitement in the air. The Messiah is coming! All of those prophecies will soon come to pass. All of the despair is in the past; yet hopes and dreams are in the future for God's special people. The solid fulfillment of destiny on the Father's part was about to take place.

A seemingly normal Baby was about to be born who would change the world forever. How could one little Child have such an impact? This was a threat to the powers that be, a threat to the status quo of the world at that time. It must not happen! An order was sent by the king that every boy child was to be put to death; and so it was done. But God's will and purposes are stronger than His adversaries! The Baby and His parents escaped unharmed, while thousands were butchered mercilessly. This Baby grew and began to astonish those around Him with His gifts. Many in the established Church saw His new ways as being too threatening to their traditions, and so destroyed Him.

We live in another soon-to-be-famous historical time. For those who believe, there is a sense of excitement in the air. The Messiah is coming — again! All of those prophecies will soon come to pass. All of the despair is in the past; yet hopes and dreams are in the future for God's special people. The solid fulfillment of destiny on the Father's part is about to take place. Could it be that He will again use a baby, or babies? Why is this generation of children under unprecedented attack in the history of the world? Why are they destroyed by the hundreds of thousands before they are even born?

Could it be that the adversary knows the importance of this next generation and is planting deception in a world which knows better than to repeat the atrocities of the past; a world that is "too civilized" for those things to happen in again? Whatever the reason, children are prey to many things seeking to divert them from any sense of purpose or destiny. Statistics reveal alarming rates of sexual, physical and emotional child abuse, and even child suicide. We hear the reports, but dwell in apathy. What does it all mean, and who cares anyway?

As the return of our Lord approaches, there must be preparation as never before. People must know of His imminent return; yet who will tell them? Christ said, "A little child shall lead them."

We have a vision: an army of little children rising fearlessly from our midst. This is an army motivated by simple faith — and a personal friendship with the King of the Universe — Jesus Christ. He will empower and lead them in simple obedience to accomplish all of His purposes before His final return. Just as when He first came, He says: "Come and follow Me." Today's children are tomorrow's future.

This book reflects a desire to see child-like faith reach its full potential. Gone should be the days when children sit silently with hands folded for eighteen years, until they can contribute something worthwhile as adults. They have gifts and talents to develop *now* as God empowers them.

There are many useful "canned lessons" available for Christian education. Some of these make excellent back-up and resource material, but what children need is individual oversight and direction. Someone with a gift for helping them find their gifts is needed. You can help them to see what they can do for God now! They will grow in that and be much more mature in the faith than most parents ever had an opportunity to be.

Our young babies will shape our future in the purposes of God in mighty ways if we begin to equip them now, not waiting until they are all grown up and loaded with other responsibilities.

This book begins with a look at Dian's life, and at how she learned to listen to the Lord for her lessons, not using ideas books. She began, knowing nothing about children's ministry, yet the Lord has given her many creative stories and songs. He can do the same for you! This book will help you to see your family differently and will bless you even if you never work in formal children's ministry.

Who has all the skills needed to do a perfect job of teaching children? No one! But often we feel inadequate to the task, yet plod along from one meeting to the next. It is our desire to help you to be a better equipper and to enjoy it at the same time. As your walk with the Lord develops and you see yourself as a disciple walking at Jesus' side, you will see things from a different perspective.

He will help you see the enormous potential that each individual child has, and how to help him or her grow.

Dian also talks about ministry to the individual hurts that children have suffered. Why should they wait to become adults before they have inner healing for things that happened in childhood, when they can go to the Lord and receive it now? You can learn to teach them how.

Besides challenging your own relationship with the Lord, this book helps you see the special value of the children with whom you work. It also focuses on suggestions for activities with children's groups and families. There are many ideas for ministry included here, but it is not intended to be an "ideas" book. The "idea" is to discover how to seek the Lord and have Him be your source and supply of endless brand-new resources completely unique to you and Him.

May you experience His presence as you read. May you embark on a whole new series of ADVENTURES in your ministry as one of His kids. We are all children in His eyes; so enjoy not knowing all the answers, but getting some real answers from Him.

Mr. Hugga-Wugga (Barry Layton)

Preface

This is a book for everyone who recognizes the need for ministry to children. Dian Layton shares how she began working in this area, and how the Lord began to give her stories and creative ideas. She also shares her burden to see ministry, not just **to** children, but **of** children! She believes that God wants to raise up an army of children in every local church.

There is a special chapter for parents. There are words of challenge to pastors and church leaders. There are pages filled with exciting ideas for children's meetings, camps, family events, and community outreach. And there is a chapter set aside to minister to people who struggle with feelings of inadequacy — in any area of ministry.

Contents

Chapter One

The History of Hugga-Wugga

"For you see your calling, brethren, that not many wise according to the flesh, not many mighty, not many noble, are called. But God has chosen the foolish things of the world to put to shame the wise, and God has chosen the weak things of the world to put to shame the things which are mighty; and the base things of the world and the things which are despised God has chosen ... that no flesh should glory in His presence" (1 Cor. 1:26-29).

If you had asked me when I was a little girl what I wanted to be when I grew up, my answer would have been, "I want to work with children." I wanted to be a teacher, or to work in an orphanage.

I was raised on a farm near Olds, Alberta. I spent hours in my room — dreaming. I would write poetry, and draw pictures, and make up songs. My own life is a testimony of how God's destiny for a person is within them. Even though I didn't give my life to the Lord until I was twenty-one years old, His call was on me as a child. *Oh, that parents would pray for their children! If they would know what God had for their sons and daughters in the future, and then do all that they could to help those children prepare!*

My parents took us to a denominational church. I was bored in Sunday School, and quite often was guilty of trying to "liven things up" a bit! (I feel sorry for the teachers who worked with me!) I heard about God, and how Jesus had died on the cross, but it was never a personal kind of thing. I arrived at the conclusion that if there were a God, He didn't have time for me, and that Jesus had died on the cross as a sort of mass project for the world. If you were good enough, you went to Heaven. As the years went on, I even quit believing in that.

As a teenager, I became very rebellious. A growing sense of emptiness gnawed at my heart. What was life all about? You were born, went to school, grew up, raised a family, became old, and died! The emptiness grew. Why bother?! Why not just live for today, and have as much fun as possible? Two weeks into my twelfth grade year at high school, I put my stack of books on the principal's desk and walked out. The next few years were spent in the "big city" of Calgary. I took some training and became an interior designer. I got a good job in a drapery store and began to make a substantial amount of money. For a while I was happy. Then the emptiness returned — this time even stronger. I began to go out every night and became involved in one negative relationship after another.

At night I would lie in bed as thoughts of the future tormented me. It was all so empty. Thoughts of death plagued my mind. What happened when a person died? Somehow I had a feeling that death wasn't the end. One evening I read an article in the newspaper about a popular movie dealing with demonic possession and exorcism. It told of the many bizarre things that had happened during the filming of the movie. I never went to see it, but I couldn't quit thinking about it! One night I dreamed that I was demon-possessed, and woke up extremely frightened. "Why are you so afraid of the devil when you don't even believe in God?" I asked myself. I began spending more and more nights out at cabarets and bars, so that when I finally got to my bed each night, I was too tired to think. My job at the drapery store began to suffer.

I remember clearly a discussion that took place one day in the back room with my supervisor. "What's wrong, Dian?" he asked me. "Your work lately has been unacceptable. Are you in some kind of trouble? Do you need money? What can we do to help you?"

I began to cry. "I don't know what's wrong with me! I don't know!" I ran out into the alley behind the store. I remember an icy wind was blowing as I leaned against the building and wept. "What's wrong with me? I have a good job. I have two legs, two ears and two eyes. I'm young and healthy. Why aren't I happy? Why am I so empty inside?"

A few weeks later I was fired from that job and moved to Vancouver, British Columbia. For about six months I felt happy. "Ah ... this is what I needed; to get away and do something different — a change." Then my younger sister, Florence, moved out to the coast to join me. We began again to visit the bars and cabarets. The emptiness returned with even greater intensity. Thoughts and fears of death tormented me every night. I increased my smoking habit to almost two packs a day. "Hmmm, time for another change. Maybe I should move to Australia; I've always wanted to live there..."

I had been working several months in a drapery store owned by a German couple. That October (in 1974) my boss treated all of the staff to a night out at the annual "Octoberfest." It was a rollicking evening — full of music, beer and terrific food. For me, there was only one disappointment. My boss had recently hired a new man, Ken Walker, to manage his newly-opened branch store in downtown Vancouver. Hardly any of the staff had met Ken. I had spoken to him on the phone many times and we often traded jokes back and forth. He had a great sense of humor and was making a lot of good sales. I was very much looking forward to meeting him and his wife, but they never showed up. I asked my boss if he knew why they weren't there and he replied, "Ken said they don't drink, and they would rather not come tonight."

Then one of the installers spoke up. "Yeah, that Ken is pretty religious, you know. He doesn't drink or smoke, and whenever I go into that store, he has religious music on the radio!" Ken ... religious?! The thought was a complete surprise to me. He had sounded so nice over the phone! Never in my life had I met anyone "religious" and liked them.

A few weeks later, I heard a joke on the radio on my way to work. Immediately I phoned Ken. "Hey, Ken! I have a joke for you! I know you're gonna love it because you're religious!"

There was a moment of silence. Then he asked, "Who told you that I was religious?"

"Oh, I just heard that you don't drink or smoke, and that you listen to religious music on the radio all the time."

"Oh ... well, what's the joke?"

"In a church courtyard in England there's a sign that says, 'Work for the Lord. The pay isn't much, but the retirement benefits are out of this world!'"

Ken laughed, then responded, "That's a good one. Hey, Dian, why don't you come down here to the store some Saturday for coffee?"

"Sure, maybe sometime." As I hung up, I thought, "Yeah, right! Come and have coffee so you can preach at me! No way!"

But as time went on and the emptiness continued, I knew I had to meet this Ken Walker face to face. And that joke echoed constantly in my mind. "Work for the Lord.... Work for the Lord...." "Even if there is a God," I thought, "why would He need anyone to work for Him?"

The first Saturday that I went to have coffee with Ken, I had all my barriers and arguments ready, but he never once mentioned God! We sat and talked for several hours about life in general, my family back home, and his wife and six kids. The guy reminded me of Santa Claus — grey hair and beard, a healthy-sized body, and eyes that twinkled. I enjoyed our conversation, and I found myself wishing that he *would* talk to me about his religion.

A few weeks later, Australia was sounding like a very good idea. I was so tired of the sleepless nights and spending time with people who were even more empty than I was. It was Saturday, and I was hung over, but I thought I would go and see Ken. He poured me a cup of coffee, and I lit yet another cigarette. The first thing he said was what I know now to be a Word from God.

"Dian, have you ever felt an emptiness inside?"

I couldn't even look at him. "How did he know?" I thought. "Why would he ask that question?" I gazed out the window, and the tears began to flow. I just nodded my head in response.

"Well, the only thing, the only Person, that can fill that emptiness is Jesus Christ."

"Here comes the sermon," I thought. But I wanted very much to hear it. Ken spent the next few hours telling me about Jesus — a Jesus I had never heard about, a Jesus who changed people's lives. I listened with a sort of wonder as Ken told me how he had a severe drinking problem, and how he had treated his wife and six children. I couldn't believe that this "Santa Claus" could ever do those kinds of things. His story continued through the night he went to an evangelistic meeting. After the service, he went to the preacher's hotel room, knelt down, and got "saved." Saved? I wondered what that meant, but somehow Ken left me hanging there. He asked me to come to his church the next evening. Some customers came into the store, and I left. Saved? Did he see an angel, hear bells, or what?!

The next morning I got up and lit a cigarette. Then I just sat there and looked at it. "Hmmm ... he doesn't smoke, and he doesn't drink.... Well, here goes!" I butted the cigarette, and that was the last time I ever lit one. Whenever the cravings came, I thought, "No! Getting 'saved' is what I want more."

That night Florence and I went to Ken's church, Broadway Tabernacle. Florence was very surprised that I would want to go to church, but she agreed. We sat in the back row, close to the door. I had never seen such a beautiful, large church! And it was filled with people! I'm sure I never closed my eyes all evening. I was too curious, and too intrigued by these people. One older woman especially made an impression on me. She was standing across the aisle from us. During the singing, she raised her hands up high, and tears fell down her cheeks. I had never seen anyone do that before. "Wow," I thought, "she's really talking to Someone!" After the service, Ken came down from his place in the choir. He introduced his wife, Grace, to us. We all talked for a few moments, then Florence and I drove home.

During the next weeks I began reading my Bible. It was a lovely white one my grandmother had given me. All I had ever used it for was to stash money I was saving between the pages. Ken had encouraged me that first Saturday to get alone sometime, sit on my bed and talk to God. He told me to say, "God, if You're really there, I want to know!" He also told me I might not hear anything or see anything, but that if I were truly serious, God would make Himself real to me. So that's what I did. I hadn't talked to God since I was a little girl, and I felt awkward, embarrassed and quite foolish, but as I spoke those words I had a sense that He was listening.

I continued to go to church quite sporadically. Florence refused. She wasn't as impressed as I had been. She said that she didn't need to go, and that she already believed in God. So I went alone or with my girlfriend, Karen. For several months nothing clicked. I continued to read the Bible and clean up my life, but so far, I had no "saved" experience.

On March 9, 1975, Karen and I went again to Broadway Tabernacle. That evening a singing group called "Danny Lee and the Children of Truth" were ministering. And it finally clicked! God reached my heart through the music. Songs like "Jesus, He is the Son of God" made the gospel message clear to me in a way that preaching hadn't. At the end of the service, Danny asked everyone to stand. I don't remember the exact words he used, but he ended with something like, "If you want to receive Jesus Christ tonight as your personal Savior, just lift up your hand right now and ask Him to come into your heart."

" 'Put up your hand and ask Him into your heart'? That's it? That's all I have to do?" It sounded too simple. I looked around to see if anyone else was going to lift their hands. And suddenly God "zapped" me. That's the best word to describe it. I watched as both my hands went into the air. Tears began to run down my cheeks. I actually *felt* Jesus come into my heart. The emptiness that I had struggled with for so many years was completely and totally gone. I stood there for about fifteen minutes. It was like God was washing me, healing me, and putting His hand on me all at once. I have never struggled with things of my past; all desire for "things of the world" disappeared (2 Cor. 5:17). God did a complete and lasting work in my heart right then and there! And the emptiness has never returned.

Finally I opened my eyes. Karen was sitting beside me, looking concerned and even a bit frightened. "Are you all right?" she asked, passing me a kleenex. "Yes ... Yes. I'm fine." Usually after the service, Ken would come and talk to me. He was nowhere in sight. Usually there was an invitation to go and spend some time in the "prayer room." There was no such invitation that night. "Well, let's go!" I said to Karen.

As we drove to her home in Richmond, about ten miles from the church, I couldn't talk. Whenever I tried to speak, the tears would begin again. When we reached the house, she asked me to come in, and I just shook my head. "I'll call you," I said. I left her standing there with a very puzzled expression on her face. I felt puzzled, too. I needed to talk to someone. Perhaps there would still be people at the church. I turned and drove back the ten miles. When I got there, the building was locked and in total darkness. "But I can't just go home!" I drove to a pay phone to call Ken. I was quite shy to bother him at home, but I needed to talk to someone. When he answered, I said, "Ken! Guess what..." and started to cry again.

"You finally made it, eh, kid?! Well come on over and we'll talk about it!" He gave me directions to his home — another ten-mile drive back to Richmond. As I drove, I turned on the radio to a twenty-four hour Christian station. (I knew right where it was because I had kept accidentally hitting it when I used to listen to a rock station near it on the dial.) A girl was giving her "testimony," and telling how she had gotten "saved." She was crying. As I listened, I got more excited. What she was describing was a lot like how I felt! Her story went on, and she told how her sister had been "saved" the week after she did. "Florence?!" I wondered. "No way. She won't even come to church with me."

I was at Ken and Grace's until about three a.m. that night and many other nights that first month. They showed me Scriptures in the Bible to explain salvation. They taught me about the devil, and angels, and prayer, and reading my Bible. I was like a sponge. I soaked up as much as I could. I will always be grateful for those long evenings that they spent with me.

The Scriptures became like food to me. I couldn't seem to get enough! I remember one night when I knelt by my bed to read. Somewhere I had heard that sometimes God spoke to people when they just opened up the Bible. I wouldn't recommend this method, but God honored my desire and spoke to me from His Word. I opened the Bible, and began reading Psalm 40.

"I waited patiently for the Lord; And He inclined to me, and heard my cry. He also brought me up out of ... the miry clay, And set my feet upon a rock, And established my steps." Wow! That's just how I felt! When I lifted my hands that night at church, it was like God had pulled me out of a pit, and now I was walking His way!

I continued reading. Verse 3 was the first prophecy the Lord ever gave me. "He has put a *new* song in my mouth — praise to our God; Many will see it and fear, And will trust in the Lord." I had written some stories, poetry, and little songs before I met the Lord, but had stopped because they were too depressing. Now here was God saying He would put a new song in my mouth! (And He did. Over the years, I learned to play the guitar and began "writing" songs, although I don't know any music theory. I sing the songs onto tapes, and other people write the notes down for me. God has given me hundreds of songs and many musical dramas. Praise the Lord!)

Well, the next Sunday evening, Florence agreed to come to church with me. We went to the prayer room after the service, and she gave her heart to the Lord. The following week was Easter. We flew home to Olds and took my parents and my brother, Brian, to church. Soon after that Brian was also saved. He went to Bible school the next year and is now a dynamic youth pastor at our home church in Red Deer, Alberta.

I quickly jumped into my new lifestyle. I went to prayer meetings and Bible studies, and joined the choir. People approached me about teaching Sunday School, but I refused. I hardly knew anything about the Bible, and besides, kids bugged me! (I had long forgotten any desire to work with children.) Finally I agreed to drive a van and pick up children on Sunday mornings. Broadway had a Sunday School of about five hundred at that time, with a very active bus ministry.

The next spring I moved home to Olds. It was hard to leave my friends in Vancouver, but I really felt that was what God wanted me to do. I began working at a newly-opened carpet and drapery store, and began attending a small church in the community. I still don't know how it happened, but within a few months I was Sunday School superintendent! I guess it was mainly because I was so eager to serve in any area.

I still felt inadequate, lacking in Bible knowledge, and not sure about wanting to work with children, but things seemed to progress nicely. The only area that bothered me was the curriculum they were using. It reminded me of my childhood dislike for church, and of my boredom with Sunday School.

Every Friday was "Family Night," with coffee and fellowship after the meeting. One warm summer Friday evening, I took my coffee and went to sit on the front steps of the church. Soon I was joined by about six of the neighborhood children. I had said "Hi" to them a few times before, and I guess they remembered me. We began talking, and soon I was able to steer the conversation toward the Lord. They asked many questions. I explained about Jesus' death on the cross, and how each person has sinned. I asked if any of them wanted to ask Jesus into their heart, and all of them responded! As I prayed with those children that night, God "zapped" me once again. They were so hungry and open! I felt a rapport with them, and an ability to communicate. Soon after that experience I remembered my childhood desire, and I realized that God was the One who had put it there!

Over a period of time I became known as "Hugga-Wugga," I guess because of my love for children, and the fact that I hugged them! God was constantly filling my heart and increasing the burden.

A few months later, the little church went through a painful time of division. Right before the "big explosion," the Lord had spoken very clearly to me. He said that I was to leave and go back to my childhood church with my parents. I was so thankful that I was out of that situation. It was very hard on me because I loved everyone on both "sides."

Eventually I heard about People's Church in the city of Red Deer, about thirty-five miles from Olds. Some friends and I began driving there to attend the Sunday evening services. We soon felt right at home, and the Lord knit our hearts together with our new "family"! After a few months, we began holding meetings on Friday evenings in Olds, using a building which was at that time known as the Scout Hall. That is where my ministry to children really began.

Almost immediately, children began to come — the ones I had led to the Lord that night on the front step of the little church, plus many others. The adults were a bit overwhelmed by all those kids! In one of the first services, a prophetic Word was spoken. The Lord said something like, "Suffer the little children to come unto Me. I want to touch them. They can feel My presence." All of our hearts were stirred. More children came.

I began leading a special lesson-time for them, under the oversight of the Children's Ministry leaders from the church in Red Deer, Duane and Alice Skaley. Soon about 65 children were coming regularly, and all the adults were needed as teachers. As I look back now, I realize that what we were experiencing was a move of God.

Pastor Mel Mullen from the Red Deer church saw what was happening, and thought, "Thank You, Lord — You're providing a Children's Pastor!" Duane and Alice were longing to be freed from their responsibilities, and to move in other directions. Pastor Mel has a real heart for this area of ministry, and was glad to see God raising me up to take leadership. When he first talked to me, I was completely astounded. "Children's Pastor? Me?! But I have no training! I haven't been to Bible school! Sure, I love the kids, but I don't know what I'm doing! I'm making great money at my job! Let me keep working, and I'll do all I can to help!" All the excuses and reasoning were to no avail. I became the "Director of Children's Ministry" for People's Church of Central Alberta. I began to give oversight to the children's program in Red Deer and the two outreach churches. I conducted after-school children's meetings called "J-Day" in six different towns in the Central Alberta area each week. I also coordinated camps, wrote lesson plans and met with the workers.

I'll never forget the first training meeting that I spoke at. Duane and Alice were there to help me get launched. Many of the children's ministry workers from Red Deer, along with those from Olds, had come to my home for supper and the meeting. When it was my turn to speak, I fell apart! The pressure, the feelings of inadequacy, and the tremendous love and burden of my heart overwhelmed me. I stood up, opened my Bible and well-prepared notes, then began to cry! Finally I think Duane said something appropriate and closed in prayer! (Now worker's training times are one of my favorite things to do! Thank You, Lord, for Your transforming power!)

In my heart I struggled. Had God *really* called me to this, or had the pastors? Was I just filling a need, so that when God brought along the right person I wouldn't be required anymore? Finally, I surrendered my thoughts to the Lord. "Okay. My life isn't mine anymore, it belongs to You. If I'm to carry this responsibility, I'll do it." I visualized myself as a puppet, doing as I was told. As with most of my inner turmoils, I never shared these feelings with anyone. Imagine my surprise when a man of God came to our church, put his hand on my head and said, "The **God** Who has called you to the ministry" (WOW! God *has* called me!) "has not placed you there as a puppet." (Hey! Who told you I felt like that?!)

It was a "presbytery" meeting (see 1 Tim. 4:14). Three men of God with the gift of prophecy functioning in their lives had been invited to our church by Pastor Mel. Various people were being "set in" as leaders in the church. They spoke many more words to me. Many promises were given of what God would do in and through me, specifically regarding my ministry to children and families. It was very exciting! In First Timothy 1:18, Paul urges Timothy to "war a good warfare" according to the prophetic words that had been spoken to him. Good advice. I have had to hang onto those prophecies over the years, and they have helped me to battle the lies of the enemy. Whenever I am faced with a challenge, I remember that God said He would give me creative ideas and the strength to do His will! When I'm about to minister to a new group of children, I claim His promise to "give me the hearts of every one of the little ones." When I wonder if I can really teach some principle, I can hear the voice of the prophet echoing in my heart, "You will speak to them, spirit to spirit."

How about you? What has God spoken to you from His Word, through one of His prophets, or just to your heart? What dreams did you have as a child? What goals and aspirations have you put aside?

God has a plan, a destiny for every person. He has a plan and a destiny for **you**. Let His Holy Spirit blow on the embers. Let Him bring life and energy to the call, to the dream in your heart. Rise up, and become all that God wants you to be! It's an **ADVENTURE!**

"Therefore, brethren, be even more diligent to make your calling and election sure, for if you do these things you will never stumble..." (2 Pet. 1:10)

Chapter Two

Little Members, Big Dreams

"For in fact the body is not one member but many.... those members of the body which seem to be weaker are necessary" (1 Cor. 12:14, 22).

The more I worked with children and the more time I spent preparing lesson materials, the more I sought the Lord for fresh, fun, creative ways to make His Word real and applicable to their lives. He began to quicken Scriptures to me in a whole new way. It was an ADVENTURE!

An example was one Sunday afternoon. I had been praying all week about that evening's children's service, but nothing had "jumped out" at me. Well, actually it had, but I was too blind to see it. I picked up my Bible. It opened to John 15.

"Hmmm ... That's strange. This has happened several times recently.... Maybe I should look more closely at it." I began reading about Jesus being the Vine with us as the branches, and His Father being the Vinedresser.... and on into the chapter. "Trees sure have a lot to teach us," I thought. "Throughout Scripture God personifies them, telling how they rejoice and clap their hands! Hey! How about a story of a tree, and a gardener, and a little branch who gets grafted in and eventually bears fruit?!" And the story "Bennie the Branch" was born.

I began to listen to sermons in a new way — trying to glean ideas for the children. One guest minister preached on discipline and how important it is in our lives. He used the illustration of a train track. By staying on that track, the train is set free! Immediately a picture jumped into my mind of a train going off the track, through a field, and getting stuck in a swamp. "Freddy the Freight Train" got tired of listening to the engineer and decided to do his own thing. Have you ever heard a freight train cry? "Boo — Woo — Woo — Woo!"

If you ever notice me during a sermon with a smile on my face, that is the sort of thing that is probably taking place inside my head!

I also began listening to the children. It was a Sunday evening during the pastor's message.

"Sunday Strength" (our children's church) was in progress, and my life was about to change. We had been worshiping the Lord, and I was encouraging the children to listen to God's voice, then come up to the front and tell us what He said. Slowly, a few began to move out of their seats. There was a mixture of comments, complete with "My dog is sick." (So we included a little teaching on the difference between a testimony or prayer request and something God tells us! No problem.)

Then Karen Cazemeir, with her curls bobbing up and down confidently, came to the front and took the microphone. *"The Lord just told me that my spirit is just as big as an adult's spirit!"*

She went and sat down. I stood there, with her words echoing in my mind. The truth of that statement has become one of the foundation stones of my ministry.

When a person receives the Lord into his heart as his Savior, the Bible says he is "born again." Throughout the New Testament there are references to this new creation, our inner man (2 Cor. 4:16). We are encouraged to feed that life within us, and to be strengthened by reading God's Word, etc. (Eph. 3:16) If a person obeys these Scriptures and establishes a regular pattern of being built up in the Lord, then, obviously, he will grow stronger as a Christian. And age is not a factor. *A child who reads the Word, prays, and worships the Lord will be spiritually stronger than an adult believer who doesn't!*

Soon after that Sunday evening, I was trying to put these thoughts into words for a small group of youngsters I was teaching one morning. Suddenly, realization hit a boy named Benji Gill. His hand shot into the air. "Oh! I get it! That means I have a me inside of me!" "Yes, Benji ... a me inside of me." It was then that one of the all-time "Hugga-Wugga Hit Songs" was born.

SPIRIT MAN

I have a SPIRIT MAN living inside of me!
(Do you really?!)
I have a SPIRIT MAN — a me-inside-of-me!
My SPIRIT MAN,
he doesn't eat mashed potatoes or roasted beef,
But he always seems to be — HUNGRY!!
I want more! *(I want more!)*
I want more! *(I want more!)*
I want more, more about Jesus!
I want more! *(I want more!)*
I want more! *(I want more!)*
I want more, more about Him!

If children can grow as Christians, it follows that *they can also minister.* But the Church in general has failed to realize this. Children are taught to sit quietly — to be "good" during the service, while the adults lead, sing, pray, testify, etc. Many churches provide Children's Church during all or part of the "adult" meeting. I am not against that. Sunday Strength is still going strong at my home church. I just have some questions to ask.

Consider the child who is born again at the age of three, four or five. He loves the Lord. He attends church regularly with his family. He has a regular devotional time with Jesus. When he reaches age ten or eleven, he is perhaps six years old spiritually. How would you feel if you had been a Christian that long and still had no way to give, still had no way to serve? If week after week you were told to sit still and listen? *Is it really a surprise to see the majority of ten- and eleven-year-olds uninterested and bored with church?* Without God's intervention, and perhaps the help of a dynamic youth pastor, this attitude continues into the teen years.

Kids can serve the Lord!! *If the Church would realize this, and release them to be ministering little members, we would experience...? I wonder... In my ministry over the past twelve years or so, I have experienced the Lord speaking and moving through many of the little members. I want to share a few of these stories with you.*

I was leading worship one Sunday morning during the corporate meeting. We were waiting on the Lord and praising Him quietly. A boy named Stephen Sicklesteel, who was at that time about twelve, came up to the platform and asked if he could share something. He was obviously shaken. I handed him the mike, and he described a vision the Lord had just given him. "I saw this church building. It lifted up in the air, and then came down on a snake's head. The snake's mouth opened wide, and all these people came out!"

When a child gets a true Word of God, it's obvious. An adult could have said that same thing, but with less credibility!

A few years ago, I had been concerned about one of the men in our church. He had always been a prayer warrior and a real leader in his family, but at that time he had been absent from prayer meetings and missed many services. One Sunday morning I noticed him in church, looking quite unshaven and unkempt. As soon as the service was over, he headed for the door. I caught up to him in the foyer. We sat down for a few moments, and I asked him what was happening in his life. He began to share with me his struggles over the past months — especially financial needs. His car had broken down, the bills were pouring in, etc. As I listened, Pastor Mel's son Jachin walked by. I asked him to come over and pray for our brother. Jachin reached out and put his hand on the man's head. He paused thoughtfully, then with authority in his ten-year-old voice he began, "The Lord would say unto you..." and proceeded to prophesy — everything that this brother had just finished talking about! He said the financial pressures were being allowed for a reason. God wanted this man to call on Him and put his trust in the Lord. Jachin spoke for several moments, then smiled and went on his way. That man has been back in church ever since!

God wants to use the children — to speak for Him, and sometimes just to hug for Him. The embrace of a child, at exactly the right time, can heal broken hearts. When the little members are released to function in this way, they seem to know instinctively when that right time is!

In the winter of 1986, my twelve-year-old nephew, Jason, was killed while riding a three-wheeled all terrain vehicle. Just a few minutes before the accident he was sitting on my Dad's knee, and they were making plans for spending time together the next summer. Not all twelve-year-old boys sit on their grandpas' knees! Jason was a very special boy, and loved by everyone who knew him. As he was leaving the yard to go back to his parents' farm about a mile up the road, my Dad called out, "Don't you drive that thing too fast, Jason!" Jason just smiled his big smile and drove away.

About ten minutes later a neighbor stopped and told my parents that there was a bike overturned in the ditch. My Mom and Dad quickly drove up the road and hurried to the upside-down bike. Dad lifted it off Jason. I can only imagine the anguish my parents and Jason's mom, Merlene, felt as they raced into the hospital. But Jason had died instantly. That was on a Thursday. On Sunday morning I drove to church in Olds, the outreach church of Red Deer, where other members of my family attended. Pastor Les Gill asked our family to come forward for prayer.

I watched my Dad standing there. He had aged in the past three days. He looked pale and was staring blankly at the floor. I suddenly realized how very important Jason had been to him. My heart ached for him, and I wished he were able to cry. Then I looked down, and there was Pastor Les' young son, Jordan, standing in front of my Dad. He just looked at him for several moments, and then lifted up his hands. My Dad bent down very slowly and took Jordan in his arms. I saw tears seeping from Dad's tightly closed eyes. God's love and presence flowed over us, and I thanked the Lord for His ministry through one of the little members. No words could have touched my Dad that day. What he needed was the hug of a little boy.

Soon after that, my sister-in-law, Merlene, went to visit Pastor Les' wife, Sylvia. She was sitting at the kitchen table, crying out some of her grief. Jordan's little sister Amanda was at that time about two years old. She watched Merlene, and then went quietly into the bathroom. Moments later she returned with a box of kleenex. She began crying, too, and stood there pulling out tissues and passing them to Merlene. Merlene reached out and took Amanda in her arms.

As I've looked back many times on those two incidents, I have been very thankful for Les and Sylvia. When Jordan left his seat and went to my Dad that morning, I've wondered how many other parents might have stopped him with a sharp tug and some words like, "What are you doing? You sit back down here this minute!" Or with Amanda — perhaps others might have made sure she was occupied in another room, because that wasn't the place for children. I have wondered how many times we have missed the ministry of children because we were afraid of what they might do. It does take trust. It is a risk. They might say something inappropriate or do something wrong. **SO?!** If our nice, decent and in order services get shaken up from time to time — **so what?!** I think that encouraging the little members to move out in ministry would have results that far surpass the odd little embarrassment they might cause!

I encourage children to come to church with an open heart and a desire to minister. This is scriptural! First Corinthians 12:31 tells us to "earnestly desire the best gifts." First Corinthians 14:26 encourages *everyone* to come prepared to minister. I never see age mentioned! Wouldn't it be wonderful if the little members came to church praying, "Anything You want me to do for You today, Lord? Anyone You want me to hug, or draw a picture for? Anything You want me to say for You?" They would feel part of the body, and the body would be pleasantly surprised by how effectively these "little joints" supply! (Eph. 4:16)

So, in looking at "Children's Ministry," let's not just consider our ministry to children, *but their ministry to us!* I began this chapter with Second Corinthians 12:14,22. The whole chapter is excellent — but then, so is the whole Book! *Please take time to read it, yes, right now,* this time thinking about the little members.

The Church is compared to our natural body —made up of many different parts, each with its own special function. Imagine your own natural body without the little parts! How important are your ears, eyes, fingers and toes?! What would you do without those vital little organs, such as your pancreas and pituitary gland?

Church, WAKE UP! We NEED the children! They have unique talents and abilities that are necessary to the health of the whole Body — **NOW**, not "someday when they grow up."

If there is anything that I want to say in this book, it is found right here in these few paragraphs. Everything else is to help and equip you to minister more effectively, but the real cry and burden of my heart is this: *God wants to use the children.* He wants *us to release and allow and encourage them* to *BE dynamic little instruments in His hands.* Children who will hear His voice and quickly respond, "Yes, Lord!" That is all He requires from His children of every age! In my heart, I wonder if the children wouldn't be much easier for the Lord to work with and through than the "mature saints" in His Church...

This isn't just a nice theory; there are many practical ways I can see where the little members can be incorporated into positions of ministry.

1. **Involve them in the "adult" meetings.** Give children opportunities to give testimonies and to lead in prayer. Instead of just using couples and singles as ushers, use whole families! New children need to know where Children's Church is held, where the bathrooms are, and where to find the water fountain!

   Allow children to move in the gifts of the Spirit. (In my home church, anyone who wants to speak a Word from the Lord first checks it out with one of the elders, then waits for the appropriate time, and uses a microphone. That system protects the body from hearing a Word that is out of line or out of time.) Joel 2:28 tells us that our sons and daughters will prophesy —let's give them a chance!

   Also encourage children and young people to help minister at the altar. If I'm sick, I appreciate having a child pray for me — they have faith! And if I am struggling in some area, usually what I need is a "hugga-wugga" rather than a lot of well-meaning words!

   If you have people singing at microphones along with the worship leader, put a little member at one mike! Watch the immediate difference in the response of the other children! "Hey, this isn't just for the adults, it's for us, too!"

As in giving responsibility to any person, children must be told that they are to be a good example, and to do it as unto the Lord. Most children will thrive and try to do their very best. You will often find them to be more faithful and committed than an adult. And it is such wonderful training and preparation for them! In a few years, your church could have a dynamic group of young teenagers — on fire for God, ready to take on responsible positions of leadership — instead of many churches' present problem of rebellious youth looking for a way out.

2. **Outreach.** Children and the elderly have a wonderful rapport. We take small groups of our little members to visit homes for elderly people on a regular basis. The children are told that they are going to *minister* —not to look at the fish tanks, play with the pool table, or run in the halls. Usually we put on a prepared skit, and some of the children will give testimonies. We encourage the children to move among the people — to talk and pray with them. Sometimes while we sing a worship song, I ask the children to look at the people. If the Lord seems to lay a person on their heart, they are to quietly move out as we sing, and go to that person — hug them and pray quietly. Over and

over again I have watched the Holy Spirit moving on those old hearts through the touch of a child. People who have rejected the gospel their whole lives can be softened when little eyes gaze seriously into theirs and a little voice asks, "Do you have Jesus in your heart?" There is a harvest field — probably within a few blocks of your church building!

We also visit prisons, homes for the mentally handicapped, and schools. Again, you will be pleasantly surprised at how seriously they look upon their ministry, their burden to pray for the lost, and the great job that your little members will do!

3. **G.U.E.S.S.S!** This stands for "God's Undercover Especially Secret Servant's Service." Kids need to learn how to give and serve — without recognition and reward; with just the knowledge that God sees, and that they have helped someone. We had cards printed up (like business cards) that simply read, "G.U.E.S.S.S. STRIKES AGAIN!" Children would do good deeds for people —rake leaves, bake cookies, shovel snowy sidewalks, write an encouraging note, deliver a pleasant surprise — and leave one of their cards in the door or mailbox. It was great fun! Kids love mystery and suspense, and

have many creative ideas of how to bless a person without getting caught!

4. **Responsibility in Children's Church.** Why not? It's their service! This will be covered more thoroughly in a later chapter, but just to get you thinking: Let kids usher, lead the worship time, give announcements, put on skits, sing special music, pray, prophesy, preach, and follow up newcomers! Run Children's Church like a "real" church service! Get together during the week for a time of planning and prayer, and watch those children arise! It is especially important to involve the 10- through 12-year-olds. If you don't, they will keep *you* involved — trying to motivate them to good behavior!

Many times throughout Scripture, God used children in mighty ways. I tell the kids that whenever He wanted something *really* important done, the Lord chose someone *little* to do it — either someone little in size, or little in their hearts! One evening during Sunday Strength the Lord gave me a song about just that!

GOD LIKES USIN' LITTLE PEOPLE

God likes usin' little people to do great things!
God likes usin' little people —
little people like you and me;

God likes usin' little people to do great things —
    God likes usin' little people —
        little people like you and me!

Well, David was a youngster, yeah,
    a kid about your size,
        But he killed a giant —
            hit 'im right between the eyes!
All those great big men had run away,
But David ran right toward the enemy!
He knew that God liked usin' little guys!

Three Hebrew children refused
To bow down to a man-made idol;
They said, "NO!" and stood their ground;
Well, into the fiery furnace they were tossed
But they didn't care if it was hot or not —
They knew a mighty God was in there, too!

Long ago, a Babe was born in a manger bed;
    Stars shone bright,
        and on that night all the angels said,
"Glory to God, peace be on the earth;
Rejoice ye people at His holy birth!"
This little Child — the mighty Son of God!

I know that much of what I have said in this
chapter might sound quite radical to some readers.
I realize that, as in every area of Church life, there

needs to be balance and wisdom. I also realize that, while children might be spiritually ready for ministry, they are not emotionally or socially mature. But then, that is the way with many of God's people! All I am suggesting is a change of attitude — a need for the Church to make a way for the little members. God truly does desire to raise them up — the "Soldiers with Little Feet"!

And I wonder at this next move of God. We all know it's coming. We are watching for evidences of it, wondering how it will happen and who God will use. "That man of God?" "That new revelation?" "That powerful church?"

Or might the Lord possibly move upon the hearts of an abused, hurting and confused generation of children? Might His Spirit be poured out upon those we least expect? Could it be that a little one shall lead us?

"...'Surely the Lord's anointed is before Him.' But the Lord said to Samuel, 'Do not look at his appearance or at the height of his stature, because I have refused him. For the Lord does not see as man sees; for man looks at the outward appearance, but the Lord looks at the heart'" (1 Sam. 16:6,7).

Chapter Three

Healing for the Little Hearts

"He heals the broken-hearted and binds up their wounds" (Ps. 147:3).

In the fall of 1987, my friend Mark Chironna, along with another Christian brother and I were driving from Pittsburgh, Pennsylvania to Columbus, Ohio. It was a beautiful autumn day, and a perfect situation for reflecting. I sat silently in the back seat while the fellows conversed in the front. I considered my ministry to children, all the doors the Lord had been opening, and the awesome responsibility that this carried with it. I interrupted the front seat conversation with a question. "Mark, what is the most important thing I can teach children?"

Without hesitation, Mark responded. "Teach them to be honest with God." We talked awhile about that, and then I went back to my silent reflection. "Teach them to be honest with God"...

Another man whom I highly respect and honor is Pastor John Casteel from Tucson, Arizona. Many years ago Brother John spoke at the Western Leadership Conference hosted by my home church in Red Deer, Alberta. One of the afternoon sessions he taught was about prayer. He said that in the Old Testament, the original Hebrew meaning for prayer was "to pour out your heart to God." I can still see him on the platform, sharing the need for us to go regularly before the Father, pouring out our hearts to Him; letting out the pain, frustration, fears... I think, of all the sermons I have ever heard, that one has continued to minister to me the most.

What a wonderful truth to teach children! How much of life's inner stress and turmoil would be spared them if they could grow up with that kind of relationship with God? There in the car that day, the Lord gave me a song for the children that we have shared over and over again.

I CAN BE HONEST WITH JESUS

I can be honest with Jesus, and tell Him how I feel;
He doesn't want me to fake it —
Jesus wants me to be real!

Sometimes I get angry, frustrated, and real mad;
But I give those feelings up —
To my Heavenly Dad—dy!
Casting all my cares upon Him,
Because Jesus cares for me!
Pouring out my heart in prayer —
My burdens are released!

Inner healing has had much attention in recent years. I wonder how many hundreds of people have testimonies of how the Lord healed them of hurts from their childhoods? I look at each group of children to whom the Lord sends us, and I realize that many of those children are being hurt on the inside right now! Wouldn't it be wonderful if they could grow up knowing how to release their hurts to the Lord; how to walk in healing and forgiveness?

Some children have hurt inside their whole lives. Many have had feelings of rejection and fear that began in their mothers' wombs. If they are asked whether or not they hurt, they don't really know. *To them, that inner pain is normal.* The Bible speaks of our needing to bear each other's burdens and to be intercessors. I have been slowly gaining a new understanding of what this means. I have experienced holding a child in my arms and feeling the tightness in his chest, and in the spirit sensing the tremendous pain inside him. I have prayed, wept, and groaned in the spirit, and have asked the Lord to let me take his pain. Several times I have literally felt a child's inner pain pass through me and up to the Lord. I don't really understand what happens, but the children have been set free. Parents have said that their children were new people. I plan to seek the Lord more in this area. How can we set those little prisoners free? Otherwise, the fears, rejection and abuse will turn into bitterness, rebellion and hatred as they become teenagers.

The first time I ever experienced anything like this was back in the beginning days of the Olds Scout Hall meetings. On Sunday evenings I drove to the church in Red Deer, but Sunday mornings I continued to attend the denominational church with my parents. I began picking up some of the Friday night children in my small station wagon. Soon over 20 kids were packed into that car every week, and others walked to church. The pastor was excited by this sudden growth! The children would join the congregation for singing, then I would take them downstairs for Sunday School.

One Sunday morning a new little girl came in, all on her own. She had gone to church with her grandmother in Calgary a few times, and had asked her mother to drive her into town that day so she could try church in Olds. Her name was Tori. After the lesson time, the children were working on crafts or reading. I went over to talk to Tori. She looked like a little puppy. I got down on my knees so I could look directly into her eyes. I don't remember saying anything.

Suddenly, my heart just reached out to that lost-looking little child, and I took her in my arms. God "zapped" both of us. It was like a jolt of warm electricity. She began to sob and tremble in my arms. I was crying too, and my heart felt as though it would break.

Tori continued to come to church until her family moved from Olds. I lost track of her for several years, but have talked to her again recently. She is going to college in Red Deer, and is still strong in her commitment to the Lord. She looks back to that Sunday morning experience as the time she gave her heart to Jesus.

A few years ago, at a camp in California, a father came to talk to us after the first morning session. His son, about seven years old, had started to cry during the balloon-pop memory verse, and a helper had taken him outside. The father explained that his son was extremely frightened of loud noises, strange voices, and things like masks. He asked that during any such times we would please have someone take his son for a walk. He went on to say that the problem was so severe that he couldn't even take the boy to football games because of the noise! I said I would be glad to do what he asked, but I would much rather ask God to set the boy free. I asked if he would mind if we prayed for his son during that night's ministry time, and he agreed.

That night we gave an altar call for children to come forward if they had problems with being afraid. Without hesitation this boy came forward with many others. The Lord had led us to anoint the children with oil and to pray for their healing. (We often use baby oil — we're just learning, and they're just babes!)

The boy's father came to see me the next day —laughing and excited. He said that after the meeting, they were walking through the dark trees to their car. His son spoke up suddenly, with great confidence in his voice. "You know, Dad, I wouldn't be afraid to walk here all by myself, 'cause they put oil on my head tonight, and I don't got fear in me anymore!" I spoke to that father the next summer, and his son had been completely set free from fear! Praise the Lord!

The Lord has given us some creative ways to teach the children about inner healing. The Bible speaks in Second Corinthians 4:16 of our inner man — our spirit man. Perfect. Why not have "Spirit Man" visit the children? We have used this idea to teach the importance of growing as a Christian. Now we have added a new dimension. "Spirit Man" comes into the meeting, wearing the usual monogrammed T-shirt, white cape and gloves, and a glittering mask; but also a large bandage wrapped around his/her heart. I ask about the bandage, and "Spirit Man" says, "Oh, that's nothing — just a little scratch." I continue to question, and finally learn that the pain has been there for years! "Spirit Man" shares a true incident that hurt him as a child, and I explain how the Lord wants to heal that pain. I explain how he must forgive the one who hurt him, and I get some of the children to come up and pray for "Spirit Man." Then I undo the bandage, and — praise the Lord! — the hurt is gone!

This is a very simple way to teach a profound truth. Kids are smart. We don't try to fool or deceive them. I say, "Was that *really* so and so's 'Spirit Man'?" They say, "No!" I go on to explain that the concept *is* true, and they understand. Then we use other illustrations and object lessons and songs to help them begin to open up their own inner man to receive healing. James 5:14-16 is usually applied. We ask if anyone is hurting and in need of healing in his spirit man. They are asked to come to the front. We call for the elders — the leaders and parents — to come and pray, and, as I just mentioned, we often anoint the children with baby oil. *In every service of this kind*, the Lord has truly moved in a sovereign way. He has been present to heal. Children, teens and adults have been touched in their inner man and set free. Many, many families have been brought closer. Often we get family members to lay their hands on each other's hearts and pray for healing. It is beautiful.

At the beginning of August, 1988, we were ministering to the children at the annual "Reach Out to Jesus" conference held in Olds, Alberta. Several hundred Spirit-filled Mennonites from the area, as well as those from other denominations, met for a weekend of renewal. That Saturday night we taught the children about the baptism of the Holy Spirit. I gave an altar call, and I made it tough. I asked for those to come who wanted to receive this power from God — not for fun, not for some supernatural experience, but because they wanted to serve the Lord with all their hearts. I asked them to sit quietly and think about whether or not they were ready to make that kind of commitment. We waited. Finally they began to come forward, and because of the sincerity of their decisions, many came with tears. We prayed, asking God to fill them with His Spirit, to give them the strength to stand for Jesus.

And God came.

I could almost hear that mighty, rushing wind. The children began to lift their hands and weep before the Lord. Some were sobbing uncontrollably. We encouraged them to open their hearts to the Lord; letting them know that He wanted to heal them and set them free from fears. One of the most beautiful things was how the children instinctively began to minister to each other. They would hold each other, cry, pass the kleenex box around, and laugh joyfully —all at the same time!

One boy stood weeping with his hands raised straight up for about an hour. I went to him and said that I felt God was calling him to preach His Word. He opened his eyes and smiled. "I know. That's what He's been saying to me." At the end of the evening my co-adventurer, Lori Youb, spoke to a little girl about eight years old. "What was God doing in you tonight, honey?" She answered with great confidence, *"He was changing me for life!"*

Some people may wonder, and I suppose I've heard all the typical unbelieving remarks. "That's impossible! Kids are too young to be filled with the Spirit!" (And I say, read Luke 1:41!) "They're not old enough to really hear God's voice." (And I say, read First Samuel 3!) "You're just leading them into some emotional experience." (And I say, "No, I just try to help them open up to the Lord, and then try to keep out of His way, so He can *"change them for life"*!)

I want to share with you another story that happened in August, 1988. At our annual Kids' Kamp, I met a boy named Ryan. Ryan was living with one of the families in our church, the Grants; they were in the process of adopting him. He was nine years old. His face showed that life, thus far, had not been pleasant. One morning during chapel, God "zapped" the kids. Many received words of prophecy and were healed on the inside. The day before, Ryan had made a real commitment to Jesus. That morning he came forward to be filled with the Holy Spirit. He received easily, and his entire countenance changed! He stood there for a long time, radiantly praising the Lord with his new prayer language.

After some time of just letting Ryan bask in his experience, I asked one of his new sisters, Kristie, who was standing near, to pray for Ryan. She stepped forward and carefully reached out her hand and touched his shoulder. Then the tears came. "I love you, Ryan," she said. "I've never had a brother before, and I don't know how to show it ... but I *love* you!" Their other sister who was at camp, Lucinda, came up to join them, and those three children stood together crying and holding each other. The other kids joined in, and I watched in admiration again at the way God works. *The bonding that took place in that family in those few moments might have taken months, even years to happen otherwise!*

Many excellent resource books are available at your local gospel book store, books that stress the importance of self-esteem and positive reinforcement for children. Add a few to your library! We each have a responsibility to love and edify each other. This includes the little members. Words that are spoken to children about themselves echo through their memories for the rest of their lives. Too many kids hear things like, "You're so stupid — can't you do anything right?!" "You're just a brat! Get out of my way!" We can help compensate for what they might be hearing at home or school. We can speak positive, encouraging words that will also echo throughout their lives. "You are special! I sure do appreciate you!" "Jesus made you. He has a plan for your life. You were born for a special reason!"

There are so many Scriptures that the hurting children of today need to hear! Psalm 27:10 says, "When my father and my mother forsake me, then the Lord will take care of me." Jeremiah 29:11 tells them He has a plan for their lives! "For I know the thoughts that I think toward you, says the Lord, thoughts of peace and not of evil, to give you a future and a hope." And Matthew 19:14,15: "...Let the little children come to Me, and do not forbid them ... And He laid His hands on them ..."

"LORD! Make me a disciple who leads the little ones to You! Let nothing I do hinder or offend them (Matt. 18:6). Use my words, my actions, and my hugs to bring Your love and healing to the hearts of the children. Amen."

Chapter Four

The Church that Loves Children

"Then they brought young children to Him, that He might touch them; but the disciples rebuked those who brought them. But when Jesus saw it, He was greatly displeased and said to them, 'Let the little children come to Me, and do not forbid them; for of such is the kingdom of God. Assuredly, I say to you, whoever does not receive the kingdom of God as a little child will by no means enter it.' And He took them up in His arms, put His hands on them, and blessed them" (Mark 10:13-16).

The Lord has not changed. Hebrews 13:8 tells us that He is the same yesterday, today, and forever.

That means it is still His desire to have the children brought close to Him. It is still His desire to take them up in His arms and bless them.

As we look at today's Church, I wonder if His present disciples have changed much, either. Are they still wanting to have the children held back in some corner while the adults meet with Jesus? (Ouch!) I feel that the Lord is looking today for some disciples who will realize His desire to touch the children — not just have them learning *about* Him — and who will do all they can to see His desire fulfilled! It will take a Church that loves her children.

I have wondered why the great revivals of the past usually lasted just one generation. Could it be that what God did was not passed on to the children? In Sunday School they learned to recite the books of the Bible, and could tell the Old Testament stories in detail — but how many children were led into a vital, daily relationship with the Lord? How many were taught how to apply God's Word in daily situations? How many experienced the presence of God?

People are talking about another great revival on the horizon; another mighty move of God. *I don't want the children to be left out this time! In fact, I want them, in many areas, to take the lead!*

These are days of preparation. I truly believe that God is about to pour out His Spirit in an unprecedented way. He desires to raise up an army — of believers of every age. I want to help prepare the soldiers with little feet! Our churches must take the lead. They must learn to love the children and realize their wealth to the congregation in general.

Pastors, you are in a unique position to give credibility and blessing to the Children's Ministry of your church. One of the most effective things you can do takes about five minutes! If there is Children's Church after the worship service, and before the sermon, be careful how the children go to their classes. You can say, "Oh, yes, the kids can go now." **OR** you can ask the children and teachers to come forward. Have the elders gather around them, and pray for God's anointing on their time together. In those brief moments you are accomplishing three main things: The church sees that you recognize Children's Ministry as important; the teachers are encouraged and strengthened; the children feel like little members, not just like "those kids." You could even pay a surprise visit to Children's Church sometime when someone else is preaching — another five minutes with an incredible impact! Yet another area where your help is needed is in making sure that the Children's Ministry workers are given opportunities to attend workshops and seminars, or to have your church host such an event. If you do host it, **your** attendance again stresses the importance of the ministry.

If you have a time in the service when people are asked to greet one another, *encourage them to speak to the little members of the church as well as to the adults!* So often I have watched people during those times and have observed how they turn and speak to everyone around them except the children!

Here is something to keep in mind — *a strong, dynamic ministry to children is a key to church growth!* A church that accepts, includes, and LIKES energetic little people will encourage new families to want to return! John 13:35 says, "By this all will know that you are My disciples, if you have love for one another." (No matter what age!)

Most people would agree that today's families are being attacked and shaken as never before. THEY NEED HELP! They need:

1. **TRAINING.** Many people raising young families in these days haven't been brought up properly themselves. They don't know the biblical standards or how to properly train their children. They need family seminars and

teaching times. *The enemy is dividing the family. What is your church doing to unite and strengthen it?* Are the parents caught up in the busyness of the Kingdom while their children and young people are being lured away?

2. **INPUT FROM THE BODY.** Never has this been more important than in today's high number of single parent homes! Moms or dads raising their kids alone need positive role models for their children. What a ministry for teenagers — to be a "big brother" or "big sister"to one or more of the little members! Older people can also have invaluable input into families. How about hosting an over-night party for the grade five girls? Or having the grade six boys over to help clean up your yard and then stay for pizza? The older singles can also have effective ministry to families. Inter-action is so healthy for the church body. We **need** each other!

3. **TO BE INCLUDED IN THE CHILDREN'S MINISTRY DEPARTMENT.** We ask parents to help in the children's meetings on a rotating basis. If they have a child in one of our meetings, they are expected to take part. It usually works out to be two or three times a year, and has many positive side effects, the greatest being

the parents get a deeper appreciation for Children's Ministry as a **ministry — not a baby-sitting service**. Often I see parents dropping their children off at the children's meeting with an obvious attitude problem. You can just about hear their thoughts. "There! You guys teach my kid the Word of God. That's what you're here for!"

But is that an attitude that Children's Ministries have helped to foster? What are we doing to involve the parents? Some simple ideas are to have them bring a snack, help with activities, give a testimony, put on a skit, or just observe. (Usually it is best if only the trained workers are involved with any disciplining.)

God is very clear about who is responsible for the the training of children: the parents. He does not say, "In the last days I will raise up children's ministry workers (or teachers in Christian schools) who will assume the responsibility of training children in the local church." (In the next chapter we will expand on the role of parents.) He is, however, raising up disciples who will help parents bring their little ones to Jesus. He is raising up shepherds for the young of the flock.

This should be "Team Ministry," just as in other areas of church life! One pastor cannot do everything himself; he needs other gifts in the body to help him — ministries of helps, administration, giving, etc. (See Rom. 12:6-8.) Often people love children, but do not feel they qualify for ministry because they aren't comfortable teaching a class or telling a story. There are many areas in which to serve! I was recently in a church where one of the ladies from the congregation was giving two days each week as a volunteer to do typing, phoning and other administrative tasks for the Children's Pastor. What a treasure!

The Teachers

The person in charge of this ministry must have a call, a burden and a real desire to see families strengthened and children trained effectively. That person should then surround himself or herself with people who have a like vision. **These workers need not have any great talent or ability!** What they need is:

1. **AN EXEMPLARY LIFESTYLE.** Jesus must be LORD in every area. Little eyes are constantly upon us! We teach children with our lives, not just our words in the classroom. (See Deut. 6:7.) **Note** —Even those people who are not directly involved in Children's Ministry

teach kids! We are all "living epistles" being read by those around us. If you think back to your own childhood, you will be able to remember adults who had an impact on your life (either positive or negative). Some of those adults may have been people you never even spoke to, yet their influence on you was tremendous!

2. **A TEACHABLE SPIRIT.** We must be open to change. People who insist on doing things their way or the way it has always been done are often hindering God. Many such people find it difficult to take instruction, especially if the person in charge happens to be younger than themselves (or female). We must all be open to hear and respect the call of God on those over us in the Lord. People with this heart problem might read Proverbs 1:7; 5:12; 6:23; 12:1; 19:20.

3. **FAITHFULNESS.** Proverbs 25:19 compares an unfaithful person to a broken tooth. Most of us can relate to that kind of pain! When a person makes a commitment, namely to teach a class of children, or to help with a given activity, that is an important responsibility, and not to be taken lightly. They are not just agreeing to help the person who asks them; it is ministry, and therefore God is the One to whom they are really responsible. Another good verse is First

Corinthians 4:2. Faithfulness is of the utmost importance in the Kingdom of God!

4. **A THANKFUL HEART.** Psalm 100:2 tells us to "serve the Lord with gladness." First Peter 5:2 tells us to serve willingly and eagerly. Not, "*I have* to teach these kids," but "*I get to!*" Attitude is the key. Be thankful that the Lord has given you each opportunity, and "whatever you do, do it heartily, as to the Lord and not to men" (Col. 3:23).

5. **A SERVANT HEART.** This is very important. Children's Ministry demands sacrifice. Many times you might rather be in the adult service, or ministering in another area. It is at those times you can remind yourself that the Lord sees your effort, and that you are, in a very practical way, laying down your own life and desires for His Kingdom. You are just being a normal Christian! There is such a selfish, worldly attitude that can creep into the Church. "What about **me**? What about **my** spiritual growth?" I respond, "Work with the kids, and believe me, you'll grow! You have to lean on the Lord! Besides, in our wonderful world of modern technology, you can get the tape of the service you missed!" I fight this attitude constantly, but I don't want anyone to

work with the children unless they want to be there. The kids know, and they can't really receive from a person with that kind of attitude.

This point must be balanced. Most of the people who work with the children on a regular basis **do** have a servant's heart, often too much of one! That kind of person must be encouraged to take a regular break — at least one Sunday off every five or six weeks to be in the adult meeting. The servant heart can easily be over-burdened, trying to carry too much responsibility, and those people around them should watch out for them!

6. **A HEART OF LOVE.** You learn best from the teacher who cares about you. If you feel a lack in this area, go to the Lord. He's just waiting to pour His love into your heart. It's His love that you need. His love will carry you through tough situations, and will give you patience and strength. Love is the foundation of true ministry. Only from a heart of love can the gifts of the Spirit flow. In fact, loving people is the **key** to ministering in the gifts. If you really love those kids, you will seek God on their behalf, and words of wisdom and knowledge will come naturally! Ministering from a heart of love will set you free! Free from inhibitions, free from

what people might think, **free to just be your-self**, without trying to do things "right" or the way someone else does them!

Each of us has a special teacher that we'll always remember. What they said may be hard to recall, but not their warmth and patience. Someday the children in your class will look back at **you**! What will they say? Perhaps things like: "I learned to love God's Word in his class," or, "She made Christianity real, and fun!" or "I remember that teacher ... he really cared about me...."

John 21:15-17 is a very familiar portion of Scripture. Jesus is admonishing Peter to feed His sheep **and** His lambs. So often we interpret verses like this to mean new Christians. That makes sense, but I believe Jesus does **call** people to minister to children — to the young of the flock. These people need a *shepherd's heart*. And yet, so many churches fill their children's ministry depart-ment with *hirelings*.

What is a hireling? Someone who is working out of a sense of obligation, or as a stepping-stone to "higher" ministry. Someone who says, out loud or with their actions, things like: "Oh, all right! I'll take my turn with the kids if I *have* to." "Okay, but

I don't want to." "Sure, I'll work with the kids for awhile; then with the teens, then the adults — then I'll *really* be ministering!"

It bothers me intensely when I ask people what they do in a church, and their response is, "Oh, I just work with the children," or, "I'm just the youth pastor." ***Just?! I wonder what age group of people is most important to the Lord?*** *This mentality must change! Ministering to God's people is a high calling — no matter what their age! Whether a person is teaching a class of five-year-olds Sunday morning or preaching from the pulpit, the responsibility is great.*

As a shepherd to children, I take Scriptures about shepherding seriously. Ezekiel 34 is especially convicting. Verse 4 says, "The weak you have not strengthened, nor have you healed those who were sick, nor bound up the broken, nor brought back what was driven away, nor sought what was lost; but with force and cruelty you have ruled them." Ministering to children goes far beyond that half-hour class on Sunday morning! I wonder what would happen to a church if the children's workers got on their faces before God and asked Him to give them His Shepherd's heart for the young of the flock? What would happen if they cried out for the anointing and power of His Spirit; that the children might be strengthened, healed, bandaged up and brought back? What would happen in **your** church if the fire of God swept through the Sunday School and Children's Church? I don't know about you, but I'm tired of "playing church" with kids. I'm tired of having a "form of godliness" and no power! (2 Tim. 3:5) I'm tired of looking around churches and seeing bored, uninterested, and rebellious children.

LORD! Move upon the hearts of the children, and **reveal** Yourself to them! A revelation of the almighty, awesome, adventuresome God that we serve is the only thing that will get and keep their hearts.

This is my prayer for the children, and for everyone who touches their lives for the Lord:

*"...that the God of our Lord Jesus Christ, the Father of glory, may give to you the spirit of wisdom and **revelation** in the knowledge of Him, the eyes of your understanding being enlightened; that you may **know** what is the hope of His calling, what are the riches of the glory of His inheritance in the saints, and what is the exceeding greatness of His power toward us who believe..."* (Eph. 1:17-19)

Chapter Five

The Family Experience

"...as for me and my house, we will serve the Lord" (Josh. 24:15).

"Hear, O Israel: The Lord our God, the Lord is one! You shall love the Lord your God with all your heart, with all your soul, and with all your might. And these words which I command you today shall be in your heart; you shall teach them diligently to your children, and shall talk of them when you sit in your house, when you walk by the way, when you lie down, and when you rise up" (Deut. 6:4-7).

The Bible is very clear in specifying the HOME as the place of teaching and training. Parents, especially fathers, are exhorted in Scripture to raise their children in the nurture and admonition of the Lord (Eph. 6:4).

There is an ever-increasing number of single-parent families. If you are in that situation, I especially encourage and challenge you to apply the principles in this chapter! **You are not alone! God desires to prove Himself strong to you and your family!** *(2 Chr. 16:9) Single mom — teach your children that they have a Heavenly Father who watches over them continually! Teach them to talk to God openly and honestly, and to depend on Him for everything that they need; and you do the same!*

God has great plans for your family! As parents, He wants you to **TEACH** (Deut. 6:6,7), **TRAIN** (Prov. 22:6), and **BUILD** (Eph. 6:4) your children. He will give you the ability to do so. Never underestimate the power of God in your home! It can make the difference between frustration, worry and apathy and peace, joy and excitement as your family grows together.

The Holy Spirit truly is our Helper! He will give you insight and little "nudges." I remember a story from the early days of our Christian school. A teacher had come around the corner at just the right time to discover a misbehaving student. That student was later heard saying, "Boy, you can't get away with anything around here! **God** tells them what you're doing!''

You, as a parent, are responsible for developing your child's hunger and thirst for spiritual things. One of the most significant ways that you influence your children is by your **EXAMPLE**.

1. **Proverbs 4:23 — "HEART":** Luke 6:45 tells us that out of the abundance of our hearts, our mouths speak. What goes on in your heart? Deuteronomy 6:6 says that before we teach God's Word to our children, it must be in our own hearts.

2. **Proverbs 4:24 — "MOUTH":** James chapter 3 teaches and warns us about our tongues. Teach your children by your own example to speak words that edify, exhort and encourage; words that are true.

3. **Proverbs 4:25 — "EYES":** How do you look at things? Through God's perspective? What kinds of things do you allow your natural eyes to see? Psalm 101:3 shows David's view of this: "I will set no evil [NAS — worthless] thing before my eyes..."

4. **Proverbs 4:26, 27 — "FEET":** What is your daily walk like —upright? Careful? Are you teaching, through your example, how to make right decisions and judgments?

Some Important Things to Teach Children:

1. **The LOVE of God** (Deut. 6:5) — Total devotion to God and to His people.
2. **OBEDIENCE** (Eph. 6:1)
3. **RESPECT** (Eph. 6:2,3)

There are two kinds of teaching (Deut. 6):

1. **FORMAL** — teaching DILIGENTLY (work!) — times that are specifically set aside for devotions, for deliberate discussion on an important theme. These should be patterned as well as impromptu times. (*Plan* times with *individual* children!)

Family Devotions

   Children must EXPERIENCE Christianity — not just learn about it. Structured family times have many positive benefits. They:

   — keep lines of communication open.
   — tie together what you've been teaching them and what you've been doing.
   — help everyone to stop and take notice of each other instead of continually being wrapped up in his or her own problems and concerns.

Here are some IDEAS for families:

Spend a short time every day in the Word and prayer as a family. Plan a structured time once a week as your family "Conference." These will be more apt to become exciting and special instead of routine. It must become the most *important event* of the week in the minds of every family member. Be excited! Be interested! Be fun! Involve every person in some area. For family conferences or devotional times:

a. *PRAY, PLAN AND STUDY* — Remember, this is one of the most important events of your week! Find out what your child has been learning in Sunday School and pick up on that theme; build a devotional time around Sunday's sermon; or study the life of Christ. Ask your children what they want to learn about.

b. *PRAISE AND WORSHIP* — Music is IMPORTANT! Be inventive — bring out the pots and pans. March, dance, jump, do actions. Use tapes and records. Flow in the Spirit together — not for a long time, but for a meaningful time. Remember: God *dwells* in the praises of His people! (Ps. 22:3)

c. *PRAYER* — Get everyone involved. Make a prayer list. Give opportunities for requests and testimonies. Have children lead — teach them HOW! Read Scriptures about prayer.

d. *BIBLE LESSON* — Lift God's Word as the ultimate standard in your home. Give it a place of preeminence. Let older children read from the Bible, or even prepare the lesson. Younger children love repetition, as it makes them feel like they *know* something! Let them retell the story. Act out the story using hats and towels —have a "Bathrobe Production." Ask questions or prepare a discussion. What PRINCIPLE can be learned from the story? How can we APPLY it to our lives *this week*?

e. *GAMES* — Play church together — your kids will love it! Take turns being the different characters. Bible charades and sword drills can also be used.

2. **INFORMAL** — Training your children is a continual process. Isaiah 28:10 says, "...precept upon precept, line upon line ... here a little, there a little..." Train them when you're talking, sitting, walking, lying down and getting up! Be *sensitive*. Use every opportunity to teach spiritual truth.

A Way of Life!

One simple rule to follow: "Wherever you are, be all there!" Everything actually begins with one word — *attitude.* Instead of saying, "I have to train these kids," say, "I GET to train them!" Instead of "Oh, what a great responsibility," how about, "Oh, what a great opportunity!"

a. *TALK* — What do you and your family talk about — the woes and problems? These have their place, but Psalm 105:2 says, "Talk of all His wondrous works..."

   Confess and speak God's Word! Try memorizing Scripture verses as a family. Print out the verse and post it on the refrigerator, and repeat it together at every meal.

   Be sure that when you speak to your children about themselves your words **bless** them! *Children will become what they are told they are!* With your words and tone of voice you can establish a self-image that will be with that child throughout his lifetime! Don't use negative, destructive words --build your kids up! Tell them how glad you are that Jesus put them in your family. Tell them that God has a wonderful plan for their lives. And most importantly, *tell them that you love them — every day!*

b.   *SIT* — Guide your family conversation when you're sitting around the table or in the car, etc. Be positive! Have a sense of humor.

When sitting together in church, involve your children in what's happening. Have them:
— draw a picture of the sermon.
— look up the Scriptures to which the speaker refers.
— count how many times the speaker says one word (God, faith, etc.).

Make mealtime a happy time — Don't cry over "spilled milk." A simple rule: *Don't discipline for childish behavior, but for SIN and DISOBEDIENCE.* (Was that milk spilled accidentally or willfully?)

NOTE: While we're talking about discipline: NEVER discipline a child publicly. Take him aside quietly and deal with him in private. So often I have seen parents humiliate their children by yanking them around or slapping them in front of their peers. How would you like Jesus to discipline you publicly? NEVER send a child to his room for long periods of time as a form of discipline. His mind becomes a target for the enemy — thoughts of bitterness, anger and revenge will bombard him. If you must send a child to his room until you regain a cool composure, do so — but only for a few moments. Then proceed to discipline him according to Scripture, and in love, not anger. (See Prov. 13:24; 19:18; 23:13; 29:15,17; Eph. 6:4; Col. 3:21) This can be compared with how the Lord deals with us. He disciplines us, and it's over and forgotten. He doesn't draw things out, continually reminding us of our past failures!

c. *WALK* — Use circumstances as OPPORTUNITIES to involve Jesus in your daily lives. Jesus constantly used the everyday things in life to teach spiritual truths.

Teach your children how to make right decisions — don't do it for them all the time.

Encourage spiritual games — play church; dolls preaching to their neighbors, etc.

Plan surprise blessings for saints and the pastor!

Plan family outreaches such as visiting a shut-in person or inviting an unsaved friend to supper.

It is so important that your family feels that they are a vital part of your ministry! How many children of pastors and missionaries have grown up bitter and resentful because the work of the Lord seemed more important to their parents than they did?! *Kids must feel that this is "our" ministry, not just Mom and/or Dad's. They must also have regular times when they have their parents all to themselves!* When Mom and/or Dad must go out for an evening or weekend or lengthy time of ministry, get the children to lay hands on them and send them forth! This again helps them to feel part of what is happening. Instead of feeling resentful, this helps them to realize the importance of what Mom and Dad are doing for the Lord.

d. *LIE DOWN* — Don't just send your kids to bed. This can be a very precious time spent together. Pray for any concerns on their hearts; any worries or fears, tests tomorrow, or other requests. Reassure them of your love and God's love. Your children will treasure those moments all their lives.

Encourage them in their personal relationships with the Lord — to have a personal time of prayer and Bible reading — but as they grow older, don't stop being there for your special time together!

Bless your children as they sleep. Pray down God's protection, peace and grace upon their lives.

e. *GET UP* — What do your children hear first thing in the morning? God has given us plenty of instruction in this area. (See Ps. 5:3, etc.) How great for kids to wake up hearing Dad praising the Lord in the shower and Mom singing "This is the Day" as she flips pancakes! You can CREATE an atmosphere of praise. Teach your children through your example to greet each new day with FAITH, EXPECTANCY and a THANKFUL HEART!

Each morning read a portion of Scripture, have prayer for each family member, give each other a big hug, and go your way rejoicing!

Realize the worth of your child. Don't take him for granted and just get used to having him around. *That life is a gift to you from God! And you have the biggest role to play in his development for God.* Ministry will come and go. People will come and go. Job opportunities will come and go. Your life's greatest achievement will be to have your children standing with you in Heaven someday!

Believe in God's power in you. Be determined that nothing will hold you back from accomplishing, with excellence, what God has called you to do. *GRACE* is "THE GOD-GIVEN ABILITY TO *DO* WHAT HE HAS CALLED YOU TO DO!"

Begin NOW! It's never too late. God can heal past hurts and mistakes. Perhaps you need to go to your children and say, "I'm sorry. I've been disobeying God's Word concerning you." Have your children lay hands on you and pray for you.

"...I will walk within my house with a perfect heart" (Ps. 101:2).

Chapter Six

The "Program"

"I was glad when they said to me, 'Let us go into the house of the Lord' " (Ps. 122:1).

The children in your local body should love to go to church! What happens at church must be exciting. It must be a place where kids want to bring their friends. Is Jesus boring? Of course not! But what kind of Jesus do the children see — in the Bible lesson time, in the singing and worship time, in the activity time? The program and the leaders must be reflections of the true Jesus. It just stands to reason in a child's mind that if church is boring, so is Jesus, and vice versa.

In another chapter, we will get into what to teach kids. In this chapter we will take a look at how. I have listed five basic principles that I see that Jesus used in His ministry, and suggested ways those principles can be incorporated into your church "program."

1. **JESUS LOVES ME.**   Whenever I am about to minister to a group of children, I pray, "Lord, give me their hearts." If I have their hearts, I have their attention, and they will learn from me. God has given me a great love for kids, and they feel it. Often I feel inadequate, but I love the kids. And what's in my heart comes out!

   People who teach the same group of children regularly have a special opportunity to show those lambs the Shepherd's love. The classroom atmosphere, the amount of preparation, the attempts to know names (and birthdays) are just some of the areas that speak loudly to a child of his importance.

   I work on a very part-time basis at a large institution for mentally handicapped people, where my husband, Barry, is one of two chaplains. There are over one thousand residents, all with differing levels of handicaps. I take my guitar and sing on the different units, as well as helping with church services there. The other chaplain, Stuart Fraser, has impressed me with his ability to remember names. I have sat in his office and watched the number of people who come by for a word of encouragement, a hug, and a short prayer. One day I asked Stuart how he ever managed to know so many of their names. His answer has continually convicted me of how important this really is. He said, "Jesus knows each of our names. I represent the Lord here. Knowing their names is part of my job."

If you struggle in this area, ask for the Lord's help — I know He is willing to give it! Try different techniques, such as writing names down in a notebook. Another helpful idea is what I often use when I meet a new group of kids. I call it "the Name Game." We go down each row of children. The first child says his/her name. We all repeat it. The second child says his name. We go back to the first name and say it, then the second. The third child says his name. We repeat the first, second, and now third name, and so on. If it is a reasonably small group, and there is adequate time, I have the kids move to different chairs (scramble) and we see if we can all still say their names.

Do you remember how important your birthday was when you were a child? Think about it! It is the one day of the year when a child feels especially important. A wise teacher will recognize the significance of birthdays and find creative ways to acknowledge them. One way is to have the children come forward who had a birthday during a given week. Sing a happy birthday song to them and have other children come up and pray for each one individually. Another idea is to have some special privilege that goes to the birthday person, or a wonderful bag of "treasures" that they get to reach into for some little prize.

Showing Jesus' love means taking time to listen. This can be extremely difficult when there are dozens of little mouths moving at the same time, and many little hands tugging at your clothes — all vying for your attention. Try to make a time for sharing, when each child who wants to can briefly tell you and the other children what is so very important and exciting. (Testimony time!) Try to be available after the class for that child who stays back, hoping for a few moments of your time. In the foyer after church, when there are so many people to talk to, be careful not to shut out or brush aside that little pair of eyes trying to catch yours. Get down on your knees and look into their eyes when they're talking. Give them your undivided attention, just for those few moments —

and you can affect that little person for life! I wonder how many children have struggled to be heard by their parents and teachers?

When I hear a parent complaining about his teenager, "I don't know what's wrong! He just won't talk to me!" I want to respond, "Did you listen when he tried to?"

2. **JESUS IS EXCITING AND FUN! I think that** Jesus laughed a lot. When I imagine Him with children, I see sparkling eyes and arms ready to lift up and hug. I see Him running and playing, and then gathering those little people close around Him to hear stories of the Kingdom.

I have a bit of a reputation for telling jokes and making puns, and, believe it or not, I often feel anointed when I'm doing so! The Lord really does quicken my mind and help me to play with words. I was encouraged recently to hear that in the original Greek and Hebrew of the Bible there is much humor and play on words. One of my favorite "ice breakers" is "job jokes." The kids give me an occupation, and I tell them a joke. The more I do this, the easier and more fun it becomes! Here are a few examples.

Lawyer: Everyone kept getting on my case.
Photographer: Nothing ever developed; get the picture?
Author: It was a novel idea, until someone threw the book at me!
Fruit Company: I got canned; it was the pits anyway.

Of course, young children don't catch the meaning of most of such jokes, and I throw in a few simple ones for them, but the older kids and adults love it. At camps, trying to stump me with a job becomes a favorite past time! Kids need to laugh. A merry heart really does do good like a medicine (Prov. 17:22). This kind of humor doesn't hurt anyone. It challenges imaginations and encourages creativity! I'll always remember one boy about nine years old who stayed back after the other kids had left one morning at camp. "Will you teach me how to tell jokes like that?" So we had a little workshop right there!

I have found over and over again that as the children laugh, their hearts begin to open up, the barriers fall away, and we can really begin to communicate. If the person teaching the class finds this sort of thing difficult, they can have a guest come in with the "joke of the week," or a puppet who visits regularly and loves to stump the kids on riddles; or they can allow a few of the children to share their favorite jokes.

3. **JESUS DIDN'T JUST TALK!** Take a moment and dig back into your memory treasure chest of sermons ùthe farther back the better. What sermon do you remember? ... (C'mon, do it!) We retain a small percentage of what we **hear**, a greater percentage of what we **see**, and the greatest percentage of what we **do**. I try to put this into practice whenever I am teaching children. If mommy asks, "What did you learn in Children's Church today?" and the child can't answer, I have failed. I have succeeded if the child can tell mommy, especially using his own words, not just rehearsing the theme or memory verse. You probably remember that specific sermon because the speaker made you **see** it (either through some dramatic illustration or just in your imagination), and/or better yet, made you **feel** it — that it was something you could do or be.

Drama, pantomime, object lessons, and story-telling are not something new to the Church. The Old and New Testaments are filled with these, and Jesus is our greatest Example. His whole life was a drama, filled with symbolism. His sermons were often allegories that would capture the imaginations of every age group (and they still do). When He said things like, "Consider the lilies of the field..." I believe there were lilies there! He used everyday, simple illustrations to teach profound truths, and His lessons could be applied and put into practice. "Go, and do likewise...."

When I teach the stories and principles from God's Word, I want the children to hear, see and experience them. Often I use role play, but even if the children cannot participate, I want them to **feel** as though they are! I tell them that God has given them a special gift called their imagination — it's like having a television in their heads! As I tell the story, they make the pictures. I use a variety of voice inflections, sometimes special lighting (just turn off the lights and put a colored transparency on an overhead projector for a spotlight), music, and very often wear a hat or piece of fabric for each character. Together we have been on many wonderful adventures — in the den of lions with Daniel; up in the tree with Zaccheus; on the stormy sea with Paul...

This all comes very naturally to children. It is only as we "grow up" that imagining becomes difficult. Jesus said in Matthew 11:25 that many truths were hidden from the wise, clever, educated people and revealed to the babes — the unlearned and unskilled. *"Lord! Help me to become as a child, so that I might better understand the marvelous truths of Your Kingdom!"*

4. **JESUS WAS A STRONG LEADER** None of the disciples ever questioned who was in charge. Jesus was a strong and firm leader.

Discipline is a must when working with children. They will continually explore the boundaries. Only when they find those boundaries to be consistent and enforced will they truly respect and respond to the authority figure in charge — whether this is at home or in a classroom setting.

Many children's ministries begin each meeting by defining the rules. In some cases, this might be appropriate, but I feel it is much better to begin the meeting with fun and action. Remember, as soon as you set boundaries, the children will challenge those boundaries — so, instead of focusing the meeting on what the children can't do, focus on Jesus and the fun it is to be in His Presence!

The best method I know for controlling a room full of children is to keep things moving and exciting. Another is to motivate good behavior. Being attentive, responsive and obedient is worth it, because small prizes are rewarded! Sometimes a helper will roam about the room, slipping jelly beans into the hands of children who are being attentive. Children are picked to help with an activity by their behavior (either good or improved), and a small number are chosen each week to go for ice cream with the teacher next Saturday. A list is kept to ensure that every child eventually gets his turn. Is this bribery? No! (See Rev. 2:17, 26-28; 3:21.) God rewards right actions!

In all of this, do expect kids to act like kids! There *will* be fidgeting and moving around. I never mind that! Sometimes the child who is sitting quietly is there only in body, and his mind is far away, while the one who just can't sit still is learning and enjoying the class immensely!

I like to use "cheers" to get the children's attention. If I am trying to gather them back after an activity, or to help them focus after a funny skit, I use a variety of the following cheers.

You shout:	**The children shout:**
Attent-	SHUN!
Praise the -	LORD!
Hallelu -	JAH!

Glory to -	GOD!
I love -	JESUS!
Please sit -	DOWN!
Please stand -	UP!

When trying to make sure your time with the children is decent and in order, keep in mind — what do you respond to? Loving encouragement or gruff commands? Don't use your position of authority to "lord" it over the children. Don't say, "You have to obey me! I'm in charge!" *True respect for any leader is* **won**, *not demanded.*

It is so necessary to be *sensitive* to each child. Why did he act that way? What needs does he have? That little "problem person" would probably really appreciate spending some time with you after school one day this week, or going out together for lunch. Of course, this must be done with wisdom. The child (or his peers) must not get the impression that misbehaving brings such positive results! But do make room in your schedule to spend time with individual children who need it — you will be pleasantly surprised at their changed attitudes in class!

And please keep in mind that Jesus was, and still is, the ultimate Leader! One moment in His

Presence will have more impact in the lives of children than all of our great teaching techniques, games or stories will ever have.

5. **JESUS TAUGHT THE MULTITUDES.** At a time when the enemy is attacking and dividing the family, I often question what the Church is doing to bring it together. We attend church as a family — kids here, teens over there, and adults in the sanctuary. We have family camps — often with segregated age groups. I have observed "family" nights where again the kids are with their friends playing and running around the church; the teens are huddled in small groupings, and the adults are drinking coffee together. There is such a need for kids and parents to learn how to have fun together! We must make room for the children to feel welcomed and to express themselves in times of corporate worship. The single people need to see Christian families interacting with each other, and to feel that they are part of those families! (Ps. 68:6)

I love verses in the Old Testament like Second Chronicles 20:13. "Now all Judah, with their little ones, their wives and their children, stood before the Lord." And Nehemiah 12:43: "...the women and the children also rejoiced, so that the joy of Jerusalem was heard afar off."

Jesus taught the multitudes. At this point I feel it necessary to mention that in addition to children, another often segregated group is those who are single. Psalm 68:6 says that God "sets the solitary in families." Far too often, however, the Church "sets the solitary in single's ministry." I was single until I was 33 years old and I know firsthand what it is like to be solitary. During those years, I found that many of the singles ministry meetings I attended were not centered around Jesus. Instead, they seemed to be most often centered around trying to find a mate or consoling each other for not finding one! Rather than focusing on marriage, I believe that Christians could do a lot more for the solitary in the Church by celebrating their singleness and encouraging them that it is absolutely fine and very biblical to stay that way (see Matt. 19:12, 1 Cor. 7:8; 32-34)! And instead of putting the singles in some isolated group, why not look for ways for them to build relationships with families?

One single gal I knew had a wonderful ministry to the families in her church. Every month or so she would trade homes with a young couple for the weekend. They would go to her apartment where she had a candlelight dinner prepared, and she would spend the weekend with their children — going to the zoo, making cookies, and just having a great time. It was a blessing for everyone involved: the young couples received a much needed break, the single gal was able to be part of numerous families, and many children had weekends full of fun!

The chapter began with the concept of children enjoying going to church. In addition to corporate worship meetings, I believe that local churches should provide special times when all age groups can come together simply to have a good time. Every congregation has a handful of people who would thrive on planning such events! The following pages will give you a few ideas.

a. *THE CARDBOARD CASTLE* — The church basement or gymnasium is transformed by a maze built from about one hundred large boxes (furniture and refrigerator size) put together with wide duct tape. This series of tunnels, junction boxes and dead ends can effectively be constructed in about six hours, if the builders are enthusiastic and creative. Youth groups can really get into it! We use strings of miniature Christmas lights poked through the tops of the boxes for lighting. There are several places (away from the lights) where the "roof leaks" and spray bottles are regularly poked through. There are a few supervised "escape" hatches for those with claustrophobia, but this event is usually greatly enjoyed by all.

b. *HIDDEN TALENT NIGHT* — Discover those closet comedians and undercover musicians in your congregation! Encourage the participation of whole families and groups of singles rather than single entries. The rehearsal times will be just as meaningful for them as the event!

c. *THE WAY WE WERE* — Have your church's camera and video buffs be on hand throughout the year at every special event, plus at a few of the regular ones, to take a mixture of candid and planned pictures. At the end of the year, call the church together for a special slide and movie presentation. (New Year's Eve works perfectly.) People of all ages will love seeing themselves and their church family on screen!

d. *HILLBILLY HOEDOWN* ---- *Invite a friend, and come dressed for the occasion! Decorate the church with a good ole country theme. (If using straw bales, cover them with heavy plastic.*

They look just as good and make much less mess!) Set up a corner where folks can stop and buy "vittles." (The money raised will go to the Children's Ministry, of course!) "Hot-dawgs" and apple cider are quite adequate. We have used this and everyone involved has a great time — especially the dads! We divided the crowd into teams. There were many planned activities taking place simultaneously. The teams rotated to ensure that they all had a chance to participate in each area. Then everyone gathered together for the "chuck-wagon" races. Here is a list of happenings and "rodeo events."

i. *The Ole Corral* — We asked people to bring their rocking horses and spring horses. The toddlers spent most of the evening in the corral, having a great time! (Of course there was an experienced couple of cow pokes overseeing them.)

ii. *The Wild Bronc Race* — Everything from stick horses to mops was allowed. Races were according to age. We had one special two-lap race for the pastoral staff!

iii. *Cow Roping* — Moms or adopted moms got down on their knees, put their fingers by their heads as "horns" and mooed loudly.

The kids had a challenge catching up to them with their "lariats" swinging through the air!

iv. *Barrel Racing*— Dads or adopted dads became the horses and carried their "Yee-Hawing" little riders around the course. Mock barrels can be used — garbage cans! (If there is enough room, set up two or three courses so they have someone to race against, or use a stop watch.)

v. *Chuck Wagon Racing*— This was the highlight of the evening! We used very sturdy cardboard boxes for the wagons. (Large banana boxes from the grocery store work well.) Nylon or plastic rope was securely tied to two places at the front of the boxes. Dads were the horses — usually two per wagon. Two moms were the "outriders"; they each held one of the little cowpokes' hands to make sure of their safety — especially around the corners! (Those boxes are under a lot of strain, so check for any ripping, and for securely fastened ropes before each race.) I always have several people at each corner to make sure that there are no obstacles in the way. Race two or three wagons at once, the inside one standing well behind the starting line and so on to make the track length equal. If your crowd is especially fun-loving, have a few races where the moms are the horses and the dads are in the wagon and vice-versa! Each time there is a race, play some wild country instrumental music over the sound system, and get the crowd clapping and cheering.

vi. *Balloon Stomp* — We close off that portion of the evening by having the kids blow up little balloons and tying them around their ankles. (The balloons can be prepared beforehand, complete with string tied to them.) Shoes should be removed and hands held behind the back as each participant tries to "stomp" others' balloons. (You may want to divide the group into ages — adults can get involved if they want. Perhaps have the kids try to stomp on the dads' balloons!) Turn that country music up loud! The last one with his balloon intact wins!

We always include some skits and singing, either before or after the rodeo. Get those hidden talents to participate — guitar players, fiddlers, harmonica players, spoon players, jug blowers, and especially *yodelers!*

Something like this makes an excellent out-reach for people in your community!

e. *MOTHER AND DAUGHTER OCCASIONS* — There is no end to what can be done in this area! Fashion shows, tea parties, banquets, baking for people in need and weekend retreats are just a few ideas. For girls without mothers, or whose mothers are unable to attend, have older singles "adopt" them for that day, or some moms can accompany several "adopted" daughters if need be.

f. *FATHER AND SON OCCASIONS* — Boys can be "adopted" by men in the church, and there is no limit to what can be done! How about church work bees, hiking, trips to the zoo, baseball games, and weekend outdoor camping trips?

Perhaps this chapter has sparked some ideas that your church could use. I hope so. Being a Christian community should include much more than just seeing each other at church. We are to be a family! In this world so full of broken hearts and broken homes, let's be that warm, loving group of people others can come home to and belong to.

"That their hearts may be encouraged, being knit together in love..." (Col. 2:2)

"...God sets the solitary in families...." (Ps. 68:6)

Chapter Seven

Four Keys that Unlock a Child's Heart

"And I, brethren, when I came to you, did not come with excellence of speech or of wisdom ... but in demonstration of the Spirit and of power" (1 Cor. 2:1,4).

*"And I, **children,** did not come to you with **excellency of puppet shows or wonderful entertaining dramatic effects** ... but hopefully in the demonstration of the Spirit and of power"* (1 Cor. 2:1,4, Hugga-Wugga Version).

When a person is asked to preach to adults, his usual first step is to seek God. "What do You want me to share, Lord? Anoint me with Your Holy

Spirit, and cause Your Word to bring forth fruit!'' But when a person is asked to teach a group of children, his usual first step (right after panic) is to reach for the manual. "Where's an object lesson book?''

Object lesson books, lesson plans and activity ideas are all fine — **after** you know what the Lord wants you to share. The first step is to establish a theme, then build around it. God's Word must be, and is, our greatest resource Book. Jesus knows every story, every song, every object lesson that anyone, anywhere will ever present to children (plus lots more that He wishes someone would!). He loves the children and is **very** interested in what is being taught to them. We must look to Him first, then glean supplementary ideas from books and other people.

If there is a set curriculum which must be followed, insist on creativity! There are many fine prepared lessons available, but the Scripture that comes to my mind is Second Corinthians 3:6 "...the letter kills, but the Spirit gives life.'' Any material must first be real and life-giving to the teacher before it will really be that to the children. This again calls for time spent seeking the Lord for His input. Just imagine how you would feel if your pastor read from a booklet of prepared sermons each week! The people who teach children, as I stated earlier, must look at themselves as shepherds and be concerned with the spiritual feeding of their little flock.

Please understand that what I am emphasizing here is an *attitude*. If using prepared lessons helps a person to feel confident, and they are functioning with a shepherd's heart, then **use** them! But let's always be open and allow the creative flow of the Holy Spirit freedom in the classrooms!

Whenever I am preparing a lesson, there are four key words that I strive to keep in mind: **Enjoy; Understand; Remember; and Apply.**

1. **ENJOY** — Children learn best when they are having fun! Be excited and enthusiastic. Keep the meeting lively and use a variety of methods. None of us likes to sit for any length of time, forced to listen to some boring, monotone voice!

    Things need to change — often! Kids should enter your classroom excitedly wondering what will happen that day. Surprise them! Have the furniture in the room changed around; appear in some wild costume; have some snacks prepared and take them outside for the lesson time and a picnic! Use your imagination, and that of other people in the Children's Ministry.

(There is a need when working with children to have consistency. But this applies mainly to consistency in our love, attitude and classroom rules, which will make the children feel secure.)

2. **UNDERSTAND** — How often I have heard, "Just plant the seed. Just teach God's Word. It doesn't matter if they understand, it will still bear fruit." That sounds great, but let's take a look at Matthew 13 — the parable of "The Sower and the Seed." Verse 19 says, "When anyone hears the word of the kingdom, and **does not understand it**, then the wicked one comes and snatches away what was sown in his heart...." Children who are constantly exposed to God's Word will naturally retain some of what they hear, but how much better to teach them in ways that they can understand, and thus **keep** those truths in the good soil of their hearts!

Compare this principle to your own experience. Many times we hear great oratory sermons and read profound statements written by scholars. I don't know about you, but often in situations like that I'm thinking, "Wow! That is awesome ... but what does it mean?" It is very difficult to apply the teaching to my own life if I haven't understood it! If, however, the presentation is at the level of my simplicity, I can grasp the meaning and say, "Amen!" Then I can embrace the truth in my heart and, hopefully, apply it!

3. **REMEMBER** — In an earlier chapter, I asked you to remember a sermon from your past, and discussed the fact that we remember some of what we hear, more of what we see, and most of what we do. I want the children to remember what I teach them, and therefore I keep this principle in mind. I involve them as much as possible. Often I will tell a Bible story, then choose children to act out the various parts while I tell it again. All that is needed are some simple costumes. They don't need to know any lines — I simply say things like, "Then Bartimaeus cried out loudly, 'Jesus, Son of David have mercy on me!' " And the child playing Bartimaeus cries out, "Jesus, Son of David, have mercy on me!" (Often with a few ad-libbed extras, which are great!)

There are many ways to involve the children. They can be ushers, attendance keepers and offering takers. They can help lead singing, share a special song or give a testimony. They can pray for other children at the altar call, and they can even preach a short sermon that follows your theme for that day. They can put on skits, do puppet plays, help set up and clean up, pour juice and help serve cookies. Children want to help — let them! Involvement is a key to learning.

4. **APPLY** — "...be doers of the word, and not hearers only" (James 1:22). "...whoever hears these sayings of Mine, and does them, I will liken him to a wise man who built his house on the rock" (Matt. 7:24). The Bible is not a Book of stories from the past; it is living and vibrant and real for today. We must teach children how to apply God's Word in their everyday lives. A child may very well ask, "So David killed Goliath. What's that got to do with me?" Lots! Don't run away from your problems! God will help you overcome your enemies (like fear of the dark or worries at school)! The Bible must pass from being just head knowledge to being personal experience.

A few years ago the Lord quickened a portion of Scripture to me that is a good example of how important this is. Second Chronicles 24 tells the story of Joash, who became king at the age of seven. Verse 2 says, "Joash did what was right in the sight of the Lord all the days of Jehoiada the priest." We continue reading about all the wonderful things which were accomplished during his reign. Then we reach verse 15. "But Jehoiada grew old and was full of days, and he died..." Verses 17 and 18 continue, "Now after the death of Jehoiada the leaders of Judah came and bowed down to the king. And the king listened to them. Therefore they left the house of the Lord God of their fathers, and served wooden images and idols..." In the following verses, Jehoiada's son, Zechariah, confronted Joash and prophesied against him. Joash had the prophet killed.

What happened to Joash? Have you ever heard the story of the little boy who insisted on standing up in the car? His mother continually scolded him, "Johnny, sit down! Johnny, sit down!" Finally, he responded, "All right, I'll sit down; but I'm standing up on the inside!" I believe Joash had a similar problem. He did what was right because someone, namely Jehoiada, was there telling him what to do. And when Jehoiada was gone, he listened to other voices. The decision to do what was right never came from his own heart, from his own decision.

Children must learn to obey God's Word for themselves. If they only do what's right because "Mom says I have to," what will happen when mom isn't there? Will they, like Joash, listen to the voices of their peers? Learning must go past memorizing and blind obedience into application. This happens progressively as the child matures, until as a teenager hopefully he can make statements such as, "I don't go to church because my parents make me — I go because I **want** to!" and "I want to do what is right because I love God and want to please Him — not because I'll get in trouble with my folks if I don't."

I long to see the children grow into strong, dynamic Christians, with a faith that is personal. Young people who will turn to their parents and teachers one day and say what Ruth once said to Naomi...

"*...Your people shall be my people, And your God, my God*" (Ruth 1:16b).

Chapter Eight

Making It Happen Every Time: Effective, Creative, Anointed Lesson Planning

"For precept must be upon precept, precept upon precept, line upon line, line upon line, here a little, there a little" (Is. 28:10).

In this chapter I will share with you some key thoughts regarding lesson planning. I hope that they will be useful as a launching pad for your creativity!

The place to begin is to establish a THEME for each children's service. Then build around that theme, with every part of the meeting supporting that one central principle. There are three main ways that I decide each theme:

1. **SEEK THE LORD!** What does God want you to teach those children? So often we can be guilty of coming up with our own great plans, and then just going to God for His blessing on what we have already decided to do! Let's go to Him first, praying for His direction and guidance.

2. **WHAT HAS HE BEEN SAYING TO THE CHURCH?** What has the pastor been preaching about recently? Teaching the children what the adults have been learning has many tremendous side effects. It brings unity to the church and to the families. Imagine Mom and Dad driving home Sunday morning, discussing the pastor's message on prayer, when from the back seat an excited voice announces, "Hey! That's what we learned about in Children's Church today!" You can further emphasize this by putting a brief devotional guide in the church bulletin each week. Include items such as, "This is what your child learned in Children's Church today ... This is today's memory verse ... Here is a list of Scriptures you can read together and discuss this week...." etc.

   Of course, following the pastor's lead is easier if he knows in advance what he will be sharing. If not, just pick up on some key thoughts. For example, I wonder what children think of when we use phrases such as "taking dominion" (Ps. 8:6), "possessing the land" (Deut.) or "speaking to the east, west, north, and south to give up!" (Is. 43:6). Explain it to them! *How can they enter in and take part if they don't understand?* (This is a good thing to keep in mind also for the sake of new Christians!)

3. **WHAT NEEDS HAVE YOU BEEN NOTICING IN THE CHILDREN'S LIVES?** Proverbs 27:23 exhorts us to know the state of our flocks, and to attend to them. Children need to know what God's Word says about relationships, and how to have and maintain good friendships. They need to be taught about honesty, sacrifice, faithfulness and kindness. The basic foundation stones of Christianity need to be covered: salvation, water baptism, the Holy Spirit, God's Word, establishing a prayer life, witnessing...

Often establishing a monthly or quarterly theme is more helpful than having a new one each week. It helps you to truly build "line upon line" specific truths into children's lives.

There are five basic areas of content which I include in every children's meeting. I have listed them using words which start with the letter "P" to help you to remember them: **PORTION** of the Bible; **PRAISE; PRAYER; PRACTICAL** Application; and **PLAY**. I go through those five areas, planning what to include and how I will present each one. I then divide the amount of class time into small segments. (An outline for this is given at the end of this chapter.)

1. **PORTION of the Bible**

    a. *WHAT BIBLE STORY OR STORIES* could be used to support the theme, and what are some effective ways to present that story or stories? The following are a variety of methods you may want to explore.

        i. *"Switcheroo"* — One person plays all of the characters by simple costume and voice changes. (The kids love this — especially when I get mixed up or tired from the pressure of being Elisha, his servant, the king, and the whole Syrian army in the story from Second Kings 6!)

        ii. *Role Play* — Most kids are natural actors. I have found the most effective way to use this method is to first tell the story, then choose individuals to play the parts. Any negative characters, such as the devil, are played by me or another adult. Recently I was telling the story of the "Shepherd and the Hireling" from John 10. My husband Barry acted out the wolf part together with one of the more timid little boys. They were covered with a huge piece of brown fun fur and had a great time roaring about!

I will take this time to make a few comments about our adversary, the devil. I preach Jesus, and spend very little energy discussing the enemy, but it is important that children have a clear understanding of who he is and the authority they have over him as Christians. A few years ago, I was wearing a black cape and hat in a skit. I was showing the children how satan lies to us. One of the younger girls got frightened and began to cry. I immediately pushed back my costume to show her it was just me, but she was still upset. I went to the Lord about it. "Lord, I don't want kids to be afraid of the enemy, I want them to hate him! How can I portray his real character in these skits?"

And soon after that, I got a new revelation. I won't go so far as to say it's from the

Lord, but it sure works! Now, whenever I am teaching about satan, I say, "Kids, the devil's not scary! He is gross, dirty, ugly, and awful. He is a liar and a thief. He is destroying people's lives, and trying to keep them away from Jesus! I know something about the devil that not everybody knows ... Some people wouldn't even believe it ... But I am almost, pretty near sure ... that the devil ... picks his nose!"

The kids love it! They respond, "Oh, gross!!" And throughout any skit where there is a devil, a dragon, or a bad guy, I pick my nose, belch, and scratch my belly button. I feel it is an accurate portrayal, and it has done wonders in raising up mighty little soldiers who are at war — not running scared!

iii. *Shadow Play* — This is a simple and effective way to act out stories. Hang a plain sheet in a doorway and put a light behind it. The actors stand as close as possible to the sheet, and their silhouette is seen by the audience. Props and backgrounds can be cut from construction paper, since all that is needed is the outline. My favorite Bible story to do this way is that of Naaman the Leper. The Jordan River is a piece of string held on either side of the sheet and wiggled up and down to look like waves. I explain how people with leprosy often lose their fingers and toes. As Naaman goes under the "water" he holds up his hands to reveal no fingers. Then, each time he comes up, one or two have "appeared"!

iv. *Interview* — This has become a popular method in many children's ministries. A person dressed as a Bible character visits the class and tells what happened to them. We have had such personalities as Jonah pay us a visit. He comes in soaking wet, covered with seaweed, and carrying a fake fish. He goes throughout the crowd, desperately asking if anyone knows how to get to Ninevah.

This can also be a good way to incorporate puppets. A puppet can be the interviewer, or use an animal puppet to come and tell the children what he saw. We have used a huge yellow fish puppet named Franklin the Fish, who just happens to be the great-great-great-great-great-great grandfish of the fish with the coin in its mouth. Franklin appears with a big splash (someone behind the puppet theatre is well armed with a spray bottle of water), and during his visit, he must repeatedly go back down for a breath of fresh water. The kids love getting sprayed.

v. *Overhead Projector* — I have found this to be an invaluable tool, especially with large groups of children. It can be used in a wide variety of ways. Sometimes I use blank transparencies and draw pictures as I talk — like a chalk-talk. (Don't worry if you're not an artist! The worse you draw, the better the kids like it! They enjoy making comments like, "Hey! I can draw better than that!") Other times I use prepared pictures. Often I turn off the lights, put on a colored transparency, and use the overhead as a spotlight. It gives a dramatic effect by lighting my body and also casting a shadow on the wall behind.

b. *WHAT SCRIPTURE VERSE* could be memorized? How can that verse be adapted to this age group and taught in such a way that they will remember it?

It has always bothered me when people teach children long, complicated Scriptures, filled with King James English. (I wonder if the purpose is for the adults to feel proud of little Johnny for being able to recite it!) I want kids to get God's Word into their hearts, not just their heads. I want them to be able to understand what they are saying, and know how to apply it. Over the years, I have developed several ways to do this, and several fun ways to teach the verses. Here are some examples. (Note: H.W.V. stands for Hugga-Wugga Version, and the ellipses, dashes, and bold type are to help you know the rhythm.)

"The people ... who know — their — God shall have **mega-muscles**, and go on ADVENTURES!!!" Daniel 11:32 B — YEAH! (H.W.V.) *This is done with actions:* "People" — *point out in a semi-circle;* "know — their" —*pound your heart lightly with both hands;* "God" — *point up;* "mega-muscles" — *make muscle pose;* "ADVENTURES" — *raise up both hands and wave your hands in excitement;* "YEAH" — *snap your fingers and look cool!*

"**Be** built **up** in your most holy **faith!** Pray in the **spirit** — every**day!**" Jude 20, uh-**huh!** Jude 20, uh-**huh!** Jude 20, uh-**huh!** (H.W.V.)

"For **God** so loved the world that He **gave** His Son! Now if you **believe** in Him, you'll **go** to Hea*vun!*" John chapter 3 and verse 16 — I'm **so glad** that God loves me! (H.W.V.)

"**Behold**, I stand at the **door** and knock! *[KNOCK on the wall or chair]* If anyone **hears** My voice and opens **up** ... **I** will come in, and I will **sup** with him! Uh-huh! Uh-huh! Revelation, 3 verse 20 ... C'mon, say it again, everybody! (H.W.V.)

I simply changed the words slightly so they would rhyme. We say these verses "rap" style, often with older boys at the mikes providing the beat.

We use balloons a lot. Children who come early help blow them up before class, and we tape them to the wall for memory verse time. We repeat the verse together, and each time a child is chosen to come forward and pop a balloon by pushing a pen into it. We use about a dozen balloons, and by the twelfth time through, even the younger kids are able to say the verse. We also keep explaining what it means. Recently I picked twelve of the older boys to come to the front, blow up a balloon, and hold it. Each boy, one by one, chose one of the other children to come up and pop his balloon, as the verse was repeated.

Another fun method is to make a scroll about a foot wide and twenty feet long, or longer if the verse is long. I have usually just taped 8 ½" x 11" sheets of paper together and put a piece of doweling or a roll of heavy paper on each end. The words of the verse are printed across it — large and bold. Two children are chosen to hold the scroll, stretching it across the front of the room. Each time the verse is repeated, one word from either end of the scroll is rolled in. Soon the scroll is completely rolled up, and the children know another verse!

2. PRAISE

What songs would help to seal this lesson in their hearts? Are there some new things you could do in the worship time? Do the children enjoy worship? *NOTE: What kind of an example are you as a worshiper?*

Matthew 21:15, 16 tells of the children in the temple crying out, "Hosanna to the Son of David!" The Bible says the religious leaders were "indignant" — they were downright angry! Jesus' response was,

"Have you never read, 'Out of the mouths of babes and nursing infants You have perfected praise?' "

The enemy still hates the praise of children. It is powerful! When we lead children in a time of singing (or they lead us), we are not just putting in time! The songs we choose should not be confined to "kids' songs." Let's get in there and **worship**! Teach the children what the Bible says about this. Have the person in charge of Music Ministry speak to your class. Have some children look up Scriptures on God's plan for music in His house, and get them to share those verses with the other children. When the children really worship, Jesus called it **perfect**. God inhabits the praises of His people (Ps. 22:3). What would happen if He showed up in your children's meeting? Do we really know what we are asking when we invite the Lord to be in our midst? Often we have asked Him to come and just make Himself at home; just come and be Himself.

That can interrupt a nice organized meeting. Things might get out of our control. **GOOD!** I would rather have a move of God and experience the anointing of the Holy Spirit than have my nice little meeting! No great story-telling or excellent puppet show can accomplish what the Holy Spirit can in a brief moment when He touches the life of a child. I have seen Him do this again and again and again, but still not nearly as often as I'd like to. Now seems like as good a time as any to tell you of one such experience.

In August, 1988, I was ministering together with two of my fellow adventurers, Lori Youb and Berni Richardson. We were speaking at Shiloh Christian Fellowship in Oakland, California, where David Kiteley is pastor. We had children's meetings in the mornings and family rallies every evening for four days. About 200 children attended, many of them from the neighborhood. On the last morning, I gave an invitation to the children to come forward if they wanted to receive the infilling of the Holy Spirit. As at other camps that summer, I made it as tough as I could, telling them not to look around at what other kids were doing, and to search their hearts and only come forward if they REALLY wanted to live for Jesus. Slowly, well over 100 children came forward, many with tears streaming down their faces.

My youth pastor brother, Brian, has a method of praying for large groups to receive the Holy

Spirit. I quite often use his idea. I call it the "1-2-3" method. Helpers came forward to stand with the children. I led them in a prayer to receive Jesus, in case they had not yet done so, then got them to pray after me. I used words something like this: "Dear Jesus ... I want to live for You ... I want to be a strong Christian ... I need Your power to help me ... I ask You, Lord Jesus ... to fill me with Your Holy Spirit ... fill me with Your power ... Let me speak in a brand new language ... . Right now!" Then I told the kids we would count to three together. At the number 3, we would all lift our hands in the air and begin to talk in a new heavenly language —as loud, and as hard, and as fast as they could! And that is exactly what we did!

This "1-2-3" method works well for several reasons, mostly because the kids don't have time to worry about what they sound like, and they can't hear themselves anyway! It also helps release their faith. *Before we ever pray for children to be filled with the Holy Spirit, we always spend time teaching them who the Holy Spirit is and what the Bible says about this whole thing.* **Kids are never too young.** John the Baptist was filled with the Spirit in his mother's womb! (Luke 1:41) We read Luke 11:9-13 and explain that the Heavenly Father *wants* to give us the Holy Spirit. Joel 2:28 is God's promise to pour out His Spirit — upon you and your **children**! Throughout the book of Acts, people received the Holy Spirit and immediately spoke in a new language (Acts 2:4; 8:17; 10:44-46; 19:6). We teach the children that their "spirit man" is talking directly to God. By praying in the Spirit, the Bible teaches that we are built up and strengthened (Jude 20).

Well, that morning was a wonderful experience for all of us. Many of the children stood with their hands lifted to the Lord, their faces shining, and their new languages bubbling forth. Some were laying on the floor, weeping before the Lord. Adults and children were moving among them, softly praying and holding them close. Lori, Berni and I kept playing and singing quiet worship songs as the Spirit of God moved in our midst. After about 45 minutes, the mood began to change into one of rejoicing! We upped the tempo of the music, and the children began to laugh and dance. Soon 200 kids and a handful of adults began to dance around the perimeter of the sanctuary! They danced for almost half an hour while we led the singing. The joy on their faces was wonderful. That morning was truly a visitation from God. (It had to be! For one thing, you don't just let

200 kids dance around a church sanctuary!
Think about it!)

One parent spoke to me after something
similar that happened a few years ago at our
Kids' Kamp. "You are an emotional person,
Dian, so you naturally minister in an emotional
way." Well, if seeing kids touched like this
makes me wear the brand "emotional" I will
gladly do so! Kids **need** to be touched in their
emotions! They **need** God to get hold of their
hearts! *And they need every bit of power that's
available to them.* Worship is an emotional
experience. If a person's emotions aren't involved, then all they are doing is going through
the motions, just paying "lip service" (Is. 29:13).

Of course, how we minister in a church
depends on the type of church it is and the
desires of the leadership. It is so exciting to see
how the Lord ministers to His people across
such a wide spectrum of traditions! We have
had the opportunity to minister to many, many
different denominational groups, and have seen
God do **powerful** things — yet in ways the
people find inoffensive and to which they can
respond. My denominational background, plus
the fact that Barry is an ordained Baptist

minister, keeps us sensitive to where people are coming from. Why do things in a way that offends them, when, with a bit of wisdom, you can lead them into new experiences in the Lord?

Sometimes we feel a bit like Paul, when he spoke in First Corinthians 9:19-23. We attempt to "be all things to all men," trying to win them. As we have done this, God has continued to open doors and give us favor in the hearts of a wide variety of people.

We use this same principle when ministering in non-church settings, like schools, hospitals and community events. A good example is an experience we had few years ago in a large hospital for sick children in the eastern United States. No religious groups of any kind are allowed to speak to the children. The only reason they let us in was because of Barry's degree in psychology and his training as a hospital chaplain. We were firmly asked not to mention God or Jesus. We even had to remove those words from the overhead transparency song sheets we were using!

Immediately, we looked on the whole situation as an ADVENTURE! "We can't talk about You here, Lord," we prayed, "so we just ask

You to show up anyway! Even though we can't say Your Name, please make Yourself real to the children!'' *And He did!* We spent about an hour, laughing, hugging kids, singing songs, telling stories, and putting on skits about the **KING** and His wonderful **Kingdom**. Most everyone present knew exactly what we were talking about, but they did not find the way we were presenting the gospel offensive. In fact, I noticed many tears being brushed away! At the end, we thanked the hospital (and the sponsoring *church*!) for making our visit possible. The nurses, parents, and children applauded enthusiastically and gave us an open invitation to come again whenever we are in that city!

The most important thing in any ministry is to impart God's love to people, and He provides an infinite variety of methods for doing that — methods suited to each situation. *And the methods do not have to affect or negate the power of the Message! Let's lay aside the doctrinal issues we love to emphasize and simply preach the gospel! Let's do as Jesus said in Matthew 10:16, and be wise as serpents, yet harmless as doves!*

We call worship ''God's Time.'' We encourage the children to talk and listen to Him — not to the kids beside them. Usually I keep this quite brief, unless God takes over. I ask the children to imagine themselves with Jesus. They can be with Him in a field, or in a park, or sitting on His knee on His throne in Heaven. (When you imagine yourself with Jesus, it's not pretending! He's really with you!)

After a worship song, we spend a few moments in His presence, talking to Him, and listening for His voice. We encourage the children to come to the front if Jesus tells them something that they feel they would like to share. It is amazing and wonderful to hear what they say! I remember one boy about 12 years old in a meeting one night in Pittsburgh. He had been quite a handful that night. He was sitting in the front row, I'm sure just to better intimidate me! During "God's Time" he finally went along with things and closed his eyes. In a few minutes they opened wide and he put up his hand, wanting to share something. He came forward, and his voice was trembling. "He told me that I don't have to be afraid to die!" It was a very real, and obviously important message. I had no more problems from that boy for the rest of the evening!

God **wants** to speak to His people! John 10:27 tells us that His sheep hear His voice. That means His lambs, too! He **wants** to make Himself real to them, so they are not just learning *about* Him, but learning to *know Him!*

I use the overhead projector for all the songs we sing — not showing just the words, but also colored drawings on the same transparency. This takes a lot of work to prepare, but once you do a song, it's done. I have an artist friend who does a lot of illustrating for me. I also use pictures from activity and coloring books if the copyright rules on the inside page allow copying for classroom use. Then I shrink or enlarge the picture on the photocopier, set up a page with it and the corresponding song, and photocopy it onto a transparency. (Use transparencies made for photocopying.) Be sure to use permanent ink markers when you color the pictures.

If you don't play a musical instrument, LEARN! (I have found the guitar to be simple and very versatile!) Another option is to recruit someone who does play. Often some of the older children are taking music lessons, or one of the teens could help. You can also sing along with a tape, or just sing without accompaniment.

A fun way to involve the children is to have about six of them prepare an "air band." They can play invisible or cardboard instruments, use invisible or some sort of creative microphones, and sing along to a tape of their favorite Christian group! Also make way for other expressions of worship to the Lord! Creative dance, tambourines, flags and banners are some of the wonderful ways there are to offer up praise to Him. Children naturally want to move their bodies, so let them worship God with their whole being. Young children are especially uninhibited in this area.

When children *really* worship, it is a blessing to adults, and God truly ministers through them. I use every possible opportunity to put the little members in front of the congregation. For example, when we minister in a family camp setting, we always ask to make a presentation for the adults on the final evening. The children sing the songs they have learned and say their memory verses. Three or four children give testimonies of how the Lord has touched them at camp. Several children lead in prayer, asking God to bless the families, and to help the parents really love their kids. Before the presentation, I encourage the children to worship with all of their hearts. I tell them how usually when children do something on the platform, the adults say, "Oh, aren't they cute?" But we want them to say, "Wow! Aren't they **powerful**?!"

3. PRAYER

Make this an ADVENTURE! *Remember, you are helping to establish life-long patterns in their attitudes toward talking to God!* Teach the children about the "secret place" and prayerfully strive to impart a love for spending time in God's presence.

The "secret place" is where "Spirit Man" goes to get stronger. It can be behind the couch, in your closet, beside your bed, underneath your bed covers — any place you can get alone with Jesus! I tell the children how Suzanna Wesley used to cover her head with her long apron, and all of her many children knew they should be quiet — "Mom's in her secret place!"

Children love this whole concept. I remember a few years ago when I first taught about the importance of having a "secret place" to the children in my home church. One of the little boys, Joshua, was about four years old then. His mother told me how that Sunday after lunch, Joshua announced that he was going to spend time in his "secret place." He went into the basement, and his parents could hear him, praying in the spare bedroom — at the top of his lungs! After quite some time, Joshua came back upstairs and said very seriously, "You know, I should do that more often!"

Children need to go to God and be honest with their feelings, not just repeat nice little words each night before they go to bed. Teach them to tell the Lord when things are bothering them, and to share the good things that happen, too. (See more about this area in Chapter 3.)

———————————————

One more story comes to my mind. During Sunday Strength around May, 1988, I was teaching the children about overcoming fear. Many children are tormented by fear. We need to teach them practical ways to deal with it. Saying, "I won't be afraid ... I won't be afraid" has never helped me much — how about you? I have found one of the most powerful weapons to use is to **sing** to my fears, commanding them to go, in Jesus' Name. I have a fun song that helps, called "The Oooky-Pooky Song." Well, that Sunday night was the first time I had taught that song to anyone. Right in the middle of it, my little friend, Danielle, began to cry. I stopped singing, and asked what was the matter. "I get scared of the dark!" she sobbed.

I asked some of the other children to gather around Danielle, and we prayed for her. I asked her to command the fear, saying, "Fear — get out of me in Jesus' Name!" Soon her tears disappeared and she happily sang along. After the service, I saw Danielle on the knee of one of my co-adventurers, Bonita Van Veen. "Hey, Dian," she called, "I just asked Danielle what she learned about tonight in Sunday Strength. She said, 'We got the scares out of us!' " We laughed and hugged Danielle. Just then her mother, Lana, was coming toward us. "Hey, Lana," I said, "The kids prayed for Danielle tonight. She says she got the scares out of her!" I expected Lana to smile, but instead she looked absolutely relieved. "Praise God! We've been up with her every night for weeks. Nothing has seemed to help!" I asked Lana many months later how things had been going, and Danielle had been fine ever since that night!

We always have a time when the children receive prayer. In the past, I have kept track of the requests on a bulletin board. We would give the Lord a "star" each time He answered a prayer. The board became filled with stars! It was a real faith builder.

---

4. PRACTICAL Application

How can this theme be applied in their lives this week? What modern illustrations could you give? How could you make use of special guests, puppets, object lessons, etc.?

It is important to focus in on what the kids are presently experiencing. Is it nearly time for summer break, or is school about to begin again for the fall? Has the weather been unusually warm, cool, or stormy? Is something special going on in your community right now? Things like this can easily be tied into a story! For example, suppose your theme for the month of August is "Hearing God's Voice." It has been raining steadily for the last week, and summer vacation is almost over ... How about a story where the characters are the same ages as your class, and the circumstances are also the same? You could invent a boy named Timothy who was bored and upset one rainy afternoon, and decided to talk to God about how he was feeling. His Sunday School teacher had been teaching them about hearing God's voice. Timothy had never heard God speak to him! You go on to explain how, during his time of prayer, he keeps getting this "feeling" to go for a walk. Finally he puts on his raincoat and walks down the street. Maybe he sees the new boy who just moved in a few houses down from his. "Hmmm... sure looks lonely. I wonder if he'll be in my grade at school? Maybe I'll just say hi...."

There are many ways to help tie spiritual truths to a child's everyday life. Be sure to tap the many resource people in your congregation. Many people refuse to teach children, but most are willing to come one Sunday for fifteen minutes to share something from their personal lives. If you're teaching about God's faithfulness, have one of the senior citizens come in and tell of one of his experiences in this area. If you're teaching on salvation, have an excited new convert tell his story. Invite a policeman to talk about the importance of obedience, a fireman to share how he is involved in "saving people from the fire," or a weight lifter to demonstrate the importance of exercise — natural and spiritual!

5. PLAY

Games and Activities — Be creative! It is during these times that teachers and helpers have the opportunity to *really get to know* the kids!

a. *REVIEW GAMES* — Here are a few fun ways to fill those times when the adult service is going on longer than expected, and the kids are getting restless.

i. *Tic-tac-toe* — Using a chalkboard or an overhead projector, we play a variation of the age-old game, "X and O." The children are divided into two teams. One side is "X's" and the other side is "O's." Questions are asked about that day's lesson, recent lessons, or the Bible in general. The team that answers correctly tells where they want their "X" or "O" put, and the first team to make a straight line wins.

ii. *Cross Draw* — Another variation of an old game, this one known by the unedifying name of "hangman." Again using a chalk board or an overhead, I draw the twelve outside points of a cross. I mentally choose a word from that day's lesson, and draw blank spaces, one for each letter of the word. It's me against the kids as they guess the letters. If a letter is in my word, I put it in the appropriate blank; if not, I print it somewhere else on the board, and proceed to draw one line of the cross. If the kids guess the word before I draw the cross, they win!

iii. *Dirty Running Shoe* — Yet another variation of a well-known game, "hot potato.'' The children form a circle and sit down. If the group is large, form two or three circles. Choose a shoe from each group, or offer your own. Turn your back and lead the group in a chorus, while they quickly pass the shoe from one child to the next. Stop the song whenever you want, and turn to the circle. Whoever is holding the shoe answers a question from the Bible. That person then joins you, and gets to ask the next question, after which he sits down, and the next child joins you.

iv. *Balloon Pop* — Two colors of balloons are blown up, and the children split into two teams. When a child correctly answers a question, they come forward and pop a balloon for their team. The first team who pops all of their balloons wins.

b. *CRAFTS* — Children love to make something and then take it home! We rarely have time for this, except at summer camps. We always try to choose crafts that are of such a quality that the kids (and parents!) will want to keep them — not throw them into the garbage. We also choose things that always turn out — no matter what! That way every child has a sense of accomplishment. Since my favorite theme idea usually centers around the Kingdom, we have often made castles out of sugar cubes. The mortar is white icing, and the children build on brightly colored plastic plates. (**NOTE:** Some types of icing sugar contain cornstarch, and will not harden. This makes the castles too fragile. Try adding egg whites.) The flags are made from construction paper and toothpicks. Sometimes we use gum-drop candies for extra decoration. The kids can be as creative as they want, but everyone's looks great. We only have one rule — no one can eat the sugar cubes, but they are allowed to lick their fingers occasionally!

An old standby craft is making cards. If you use glitter, I have found it helpful to have "color stations" with an adult overseeing one or two of the color choices. The children do the gluing and glittering part under adult supervision. Older children can help the younger ones. There are many great resource books with super ideas; there are also many great resource people in your congregation — use them!

NOTE: I am reminded of an instance several years ago when a group of children were making Easter cards. I overheard this wonderful conversation: "I'm gonna give my card to my grandma ... Who are you gonna give yours to?" *"I'm gonna give mine to God!"* "How are you gonna do that?!" *"I'm gonna put it in the offering!"*

c. *MOVIES* — Sometimes kids need just a fun time at church. We have quite regularly turned a meeting into a movie night, especially when there have been a series of guest speakers and the kids have been at church three nights in a row. We use a large screen and a video, being sure to choose a Christian movie or a good children's show that **you have previewed**. It is extremely important that anything you show the children has been screened. To my surprise, even "Christian" cartoons can contain unnecessary violence. During the movie, we pass out bags of popcorn and containers of juice (the small boxes of juice with the straws are most spill-proof). Helpers are not allowed to stand around the back of the room and talk, but are encouraged to sit among the kids. Often I'm on the floor at the front with a dozen or so little ones nestled close. This is fellowship time!

Another fun idea is to make your own movies. If someone in your congregation has a video camera, have them come and tape the children. Perhaps use a rehearsed skit, or just a regular service will work. Make sure that they get some good close-up shots. Then show the movie to the kids. They love to see themselves on T.V.!

d. *GO!* Sometimes for an activity, go and DO what you just learned —visit a home for the elderly, make birthday cards for missionary children, etc. See chapter two, "Little Members, Big Dreams" for ideas. Kids need to feel that what they are doing is useful and needed — just like all of us!

OUTLINE for a 45-minute Class

5 min. Welcome; Introduce the THEME

10 min. Praise and Prayer

2 min. Object Lesson, Puppet Show, or Skit

4 min. Memory Verse

2 min. Another Object Lesson, Puppet Show, or Skit

10 min. Bible Story — using a fun method

6 min. Practical Application
— creative story or special guest

2 min. Prayer Time

4 min. Play and activity time

As you can see, 45 minutes is quickly filled. (It allows very little ministry time. I like having between an hour and an hour and a half.) In most Sunday School settings, 45 minutes seems to be a regular class time. If you are in a Children's Church program and have more time, just build on this basic outline. Dividing it into small segments ensures that the pace will be quick and interesting for the short attention spans of children. It also helps when recruiting helpers. Asking people to help with your class often meets with excuses. Try asking them to just present a 2-minute object lesson or a 4-minute activity! Their response will be much more favorable.

I pray that the Lord will use these thoughts to inspire you and help release you into creative ways to teach His Word to the children. Let's strive to make their spiritual diets well-balanced, interesting, and full of life and color!

Jesus said in John 21:15, "Feed My lambs..."

Chapter Nine

Dealing with Feelings of Inadequacy

"...Why do I go mourning because of the oppression of the enemy? Oh, send out Your light and Your truth! Let them lead me... Why are you cast down, O my soul? And why are you disquieted within me? Hope in God; for I shall yet praise Him, the help of my countenance and my God" (Ps. 43:2,3,5).

I had not originally considered including this chapter, although I usually deal with it briefly in workshops and seminars. This past weekend, Barry and I conducted a workshop for the Children's Ministry workers at a church in Calgary. I had planned to touch on the subject of inadequacies, then close with a time of personal ministry to the people. Without consciously realizing what I was doing, I began to share from my past experiences — the hurts, disillusionments and frustrations — and the Spirit of the Lord began to do a deep work in their hearts. The Lord spoke to me that He wanted me to share the same things with you, the reader.

It is so much easier to talk about the surface things of our lives, isn't it? Digging around in the past can be painful, and often we would rather simply apply the apostle Paul's words in Philippians 3:13, "...forgetting those things which are behind and reaching forward to those things which are ahead." That is so important. We must not allow our past to hinder us from pressing into the future! The verse that comes to my mind right now, however, is Romans 15:4. "For whatever things were written before were written for our learning, that we through the patience and comfort of the Scriptures might have hope." It is my prayer that this chapter of testimony will also be a source of learning, patience (perseverance), comfort, and hope for any reader who has struggled with low self-esteem.

In the first chapter, I shared how I felt untrained and unprepared to work with children, especially as a Children's Pastor! I told briefly about some prophetic words that were spoken over me, and how First Timothy 1:18 tells us to "war a good warfare" according to such prophetic words. I closed the chapter by encouraging you to hang on to what God has spoken.

This was very difficult for me to do. Deep in my heart, from childhood roots, was a feeling that in order to be loved and appreciated, I had to "perform." I had to do something that was recognized — get good marks at school, make up a poem, or win an essay contest. In my inner being these childhood feelings carried over to my relationship with the Lord and authority figures in the church. As I worked as Children's Pastor, there was always an underlying feeling that I wasn't doing well enough. I used to think, "I'm not really the person who should be doing this. Someday God will bring the right person along, and I'll be set down."

LIES! Over and over, through other prophetic words, through the Bible, through the voice of the Spirit to my own heart, God had said that He had *called* me. He promised to be with me, and to give me the strength and creativity that I needed. But instead of believing the Word of the Lord, I believed the lying thoughts of my mind.

I worked at the church for six years. The last year I really began to slip. My energy level was sagging, and the creative flow of ideas that God had so mercifully blessed me with seemed sluggish. I struggled to get new ideas. I cried often. I was faced with those feelings so often called "burn-out."

In retrospect, it is obvious what had happened to me. The constant performance orientation of my heart had caused me to work and work and work —if I didn't, immediate guilt feelings would bombard me. I felt that I was getting paid to shepherd those kids, so it was only right that I was with them in every children's meeting! For six years, I missed almost every Sunday service — morning and evening. The children were usually in the corporate meeting for worship, then we would go out for the message part. I missed hearing almost every guest speaker who ministered to our body. My pastor talked to me often about it. He would encourage me to train other people, and to delegate responsibility. "It's your job to make sure things get done," he would tell me, "but *not to do everything!*"

I always had an answer — how I was ministered to by ministering to the kids, which was true; and how I tried to listen to the tapes of the services, which I didn't often do. I did delegate some responsibility and involve other people; in fact, we had a very dynamic team of creative, caring workers. However, I still felt that I always had to be there, and very rarely gave anyone total responsibility for a meeting. Again, in retrospect, the best thing I could have done for them would have been to let them carry more of a load —that is how ministry skills are developed!

Gradually I became separated from the rest of the body. I was out of touch with what was happening, and easy prey for the enemy. Another childhood-rooted weakness was an inability to really communicate. If only I would have shared my inner struggles with Pastor Mel, or his wife Heather, or someone in the body! But I continued on my own.

At that time Alberta, with its strong oil-based economy, was in major financial difficulty. This was having an effect on churches throughout the province. In our congregation, people were losing their jobs and some businesses were closing. Pastor Mel and a few other members of the pastoral staff talked to me about the budget cuts and decisions about staff reduction which were being made. For a temporary season, perhaps six months, I was asked to seek secular work. When the financial situation turned, I would go back on staff. It all made sense. I was certainly willing to do that. I left the office after a time of prayer, of course without showing what I was really feeling.

"Finances ... God could easily supply the finances! He didn't want to. He is setting me down. I knew it would happen someday, and here it is. I have failed, and now God will replace me... Well, it was a good six years. Lots of kids have been touched. We've put on lots of great dramas. There are lots of good memories, but I guess ... not good enough."

I can sure relate to the apostle Peter! After Jesus' crucifixion, he faced tremendous feelings of failure. He mentally closed the door on all that had happened, and all that might have been. I can just hear him say, "Well, it was a good three years...." Then, in John 21:3, he said, "I'm going fishing." Back to the familiar. Back to something at which he had been successful. For me, it meant a drapery store. There is a demand in this area for experienced people, so I had no trouble finding a job. I began working the next week. My first day was March 9, 1985 — exactly ten years after my salvation experience.

Throughout the next months and years, the Lord began to heal my heart, and to minister to my deep inner need for His love and acceptance — no matter what things I *did*. He began to reveal Himself to me as my Heavenly Father —loving me, and using me — not *because* of what I did, but *in spite* of what I did! And He began that very week.

Barry Layton was (and is) a chaplain in Red Deer at the Michener Centre. As I mentioned in an earlier chapter, it is home to over 1,000 mentally handicapped people of all levels of disability. I had been involved there for several years as a volunteer, and also sat on a committee of people from the community called the Pastoral Advisory Committee. Barry and I were great friends. Together we had put on several dramas and special events for the residents. Barry was seeing a young woman, and considering marriage, so there was nothing at all romantic in our relationship, or at least there hadn't been....

One Friday, Barry and I went to lunch together. I thought he wanted to discuss some upcoming event, but by the time dessert and coffee came around, there had been no mention of any ministry together. And his face was a nice rose color. "Oh, no!" I thought, "Not now! Not when my world is in such turmoil!" I looked at him across the table and spoke out loud. "This isn't a business lunch, is it, Barry?"

His face turned an even deeper shade of red. "Well, no ... actually, it isn't." He went on to tell me about how he had broken off his relationship with the other girl, because he just didn't have a peace about it. I hadn't talked to him for a few months, so this was no sudden decision. (Barry *never* makes sudden decisions!) He asked me if I would like to spend more time together — just getting to know each other.

I shared with him about being laid off staff at church, beginning a new job, and how difficult I was finding things. "I just feel really vulnerable right now," I said. "I'd like to get to know you better, but maybe after I get through this time in my life." Barry spoke quietly and wisely (as he *always* does!) "Well, maybe the Lord wants me to *help* you through this time."

He was right. Barry is an excellent counselor and a great friend. He spent hours — digging! Making me share the hurts. Making me discuss things I had never told anyone. Opening my heart so that the Lord could finally get in there and begin to heal me. After about six months of that kind of relationship, things began to turn, and it became obvious that the Lord wanted us to be together. We were engaged, then married one year later on June 14, 1986.

Also, that first week after being laid off staff, I received a phone call from Shiloh Christian Fellowship in Oakland, California. I had met Pastor David Kiteley at a camp in Canada the previous summer. He wanted me to minister to the children at their family camp. I agreed. The invitation was a real surprise. Here was God "setting me down" from ministry ... and now this?! I had done some traveling, speaking at camps and ministering at various churches in the Central Alberta area, but never so far away! It was a real honor.

I went to Oakland that July and ministered at several other camps during the summer. There were times of God's moving that far surpassed anything I had yet seen! Children were saved, filled with the Holy Spirit, and healed of inner hurts. In every situation, God moved in a sovereign way. I watched, amazed. It was hard, because I felt so cold and distant, yet He was using me so powerfully.

This continued over the next months. I kept working as a designer, selling custom draperies, carpeting and wallpaper. I was involved with the Children's Ministry at church, trying to do all I could to help my great friend and sidekick, Bonita Van Veen, as she took over the leadership position on a volunteer basis. During that time, Barry and I and Lori Youb became known as "The Adventure Company" and we began to travel. Barry would join Lori and I on weekends, and he also used vacation time to go on "adventures."

We were invited more and more to minister at churches and camps. My job and boss were very flexible, and I was able to accept most of the invitations. At the Oakland camp I met Pastor Joseph Garlington from Pittsburgh. He invited me to minister to the children at their annual Harvest Festival in October. I have now been in Pittsburgh many times with Brother Garlington at Covenant Church of Pittsburgh, as well as with Pastor Jay Passavant from Wexford Christian Community.

The Lord has put our ministry on the heart of Jan Sherman, Music Minister at Wexford Christian Community. She has worked hundreds of hours to help us get tapes and materials into production. She has the gift of enabling, and we *thank the Lord for her*!!

_____

God has been so faithful. He proved His love for me over and over again. He confirmed His call on my life to minister to children. He gave me a wonderful husband.

And He gave me a rather radical brother.

My brother, Brian Thomson, is Youth Pastor at my home church in Red Deer. He is dynamic, full of zeal for the Lord, and rather frightening when he begins to move in his prophetic gifting! He and his wife, Connie, and their three children are a real blessing — to Barry and I, and to the whole church.

Throughout my "wilderness experience" I was unable to sing the Song of the Lord. This had been an area of ease and blessing for me. God had truly put a "new song" in my mouth. He would give me beautiful, often prophetic songs in my prayer closet, or during worship services, and I would sing them to the congregation. This is very common in our church. One guest prophet said we are like David — with the songs of Zion on our lips.

But for at least two years I could not minister in this area. The enemy had stolen my song. Often I would have one in my heart, but a tremendous fear would overtake me and I could not open my mouth. Somehow I knew that if I could just sing that new song, something spiritual would break in my life, and I would be free. There was a tremendous battle. During prayer meetings and worship services, a song would rise up within me, but I couldn't make myself sing it.

Then one day we were having inter-church early morning prayer meetings at a neighboring church in Red Deer. I was there, sipping at my cup of coffee. My brother Brian came over to me and said, "God is going to give you something to share this morning! I don't know what it is — a prophecy, maybe." "No, He's not! I just woke up! Give me a break!" I replied, trying to joke with him so he'd leave me alone. His words had a paralyzing effect on my heart.

A short time later, I looked up to see one of the teenagers from Brian's youth group coming toward me. "Brian told me to come and get you!" he said as he helped me to my feet. Everyone was praying. People would go to the front, take the microphone, and lead out in prayer. Suddenly, there I was on the platform, holding the mike. I had a choice to make. I could either pray some nice little prayer, or I could do what I knew I had to do, and what Brian sensed I must do. The only way I had ever prophesied was through the Song. I had nothing to prophesy — except a word for myself. I took a deep breath, shut my eyes tightly, and began to sing.

I sang to the wilderness. I sang to the winter in my heart. I called for new life, for the spring to come forth. The song went on for several moments, and the Lord's presence wrapped close around me. It truly was a breakthrough. It was, as Psalm 32:7 calls it, the "song of deliverance."

Healing and restoration are still taking place in my life, but I look back to that morning as a major turning point.

Psalm 149:5-9 talks about the power of singing. Verses 7 and 8 refer to bringing judgment and binding spiritual forces. Verse 9 says "...This honor have *all* His saints." I believe that we can *sing our own deliverance!* Ephesians 5:19 says, "speaking to one another in psalms and hymns and spiritual songs..." How do you speak to someone in a song? You sing it! Numbers 21:17 says, "Spring up, O well! All of you sing to it..." The King James Version says, *"sing ye unto it."*

The Lord has led me and other members of the Adventure Company into a ministry of singing the song of deliverance to people. We lay our hands on hearts and sing a prayer! In large groups, we have people lay their own hands on their hearts while we sing, or get into groups of two or three, laying their hands on each other's hearts. We do this in almost every Children's Ministry workshop, and people have been tremendously released. We simply pray whatever the Lord gives us and sing to the well within their hearts to rise up! We call to the creativity and giftings that God has put inside them to come forth. We bind every negative, limiting thought that has held them back from being everything He created them to be.

Often in family meetings we close by asking the children and parents to get together. We have the children put their hands on their parents' hearts, and the parents put their hands on their children's hearts, as well as each others'. Then we sing prayers for the families, asking God to fill each home with His love; to heal any hurts; to turn the hearts of the fathers to the children, and the hearts of the children to their parents (Mal.4:6). We sometimes lead them in a time of asking each others' forgiveness and expressing love. It's so good to watch the tears flow, and to see families with their arms around each other!

I want to end this last chapter the same way that I ended the first one —with a question. How about **you?**

As I have continued to travel, the basic need that I keep seeing in God's people is to be healed of low self-esteem; to be delivered from the negative, lying thoughts of inadequacy. In order to effectively minister, you must be ministered to yourself! You can't lead people to a place where you haven't been! It doesn't matter what area of ministry you are in, the need is the same.

We are in a battle. We have an enemy who is trying to steal, kill, and destroy us (John 10:10). Satan deceives and tempts us, and many great men and women of God have fallen prey to sin. But I think the major emphasis of satan's attack on us is in this area. He is the "accuser of the brethren" (Rev. 12:10). If he can convince us that we are unable to do God's will, that we have failed too many times, etc., **then he has succeeded in destroying our effectiveness!**

The only thing that can limit the almighty, all-powerful God of the Universe is our unbelief, our own limiting thoughts!

Every person was created in God's image. That means that within every individual there is a deposit of creativity! The statement, "I am not a creative person," is a lie! Does He live in you? Then isn't He well able to give you what you need, be it resources or a creative idea?!

I have had constant warfare with lies that attack my mind. "You have no training for this." "So you can tell a good story. Big deal, you're a lousy administrator!" And, of course, the most recent one, "What do you think you're doing writing a book on Children's Ministry? You have nothing to say!" When such lying thoughts come, I have a choice to make. I can believe them, or I can believe in God's Word — both in the Scriptures and what He has spoken to me personally.

Have you ever had a prophetic word spoken about your life? Hang onto it! Again I encourage you to use that word to wage warfare on the enemy! (1 Tim. 1:18) I constantly take strength from verses such as Second Corinthians 3:5-6, "...our sufficiency is from God, who also made us sufficient as ministers of the new covenant..." and First Thessalonians 5:24, "He who calls you is faithful, who also will do it."

Another comforting thought which helps me stand is how God spoke through Balaam's donkey (Num. 22:30). If He spoke through a donkey, surely He can speak through me! Let's rise above the lies that have held us down, and be released to be all He created us to be!

The definition of sin is "to fall short." If we choose to believe the lies of the enemy, and fall short of God's destiny for our lives, *it is sin*! It really comes down to one simple word — *obedience*. We must believe God's Word and obey it! *Obedience and faith are synonymous.*

I have studied Moses' experience at the burning bush in Exodus chapters 3 and 4. Talk about feelings of failure and inadequacy! I think that Moses felt he had failed God. He had tried to be who God had called him to be; he had tried to deliver the children of Israel (see Ex. 2:11-14; Acts 7:24-28). Now when God was speaking to him, Moses' response over and over again is the word "but." "But who am I?" (Ex. 3:11) "But suppose they won't listen to me..." (Ex. 4:1) "But I can't speak very well'' (Ex. 4:10). The arguments (and disobedience) go on until finally, in verse 14, God got angry at Moses!

I don't know about you, but I don't welcome the thought of having "the anger of the Lord kindled" against me! I think it's about time that I just responded with a "Yes, Lord!"

If you have been battling feelings of inadequacy, I encourage you to stop looking inward and to start looking up! The God who put the stars in their courses is the God who lives in you! WOW! Anything could happen! It's not your own power or ability that God needs! He just wants you to believe in *His* power and ability!

Remember Zechariah 4:6, and apply it to your own life and situation. "This is the word of the Lord to [put your name here!]: 'Not by might nor by power, but by My Spirit,' says the Lord of hosts.''

I encourage you to sing the song of deliverance to your own heart. Go into your secret place, alone with the Lord, and pour out your heart to Him. Sing to the wilderness and dry areas of your life. Call for His healing and restoration. Sing to that well to rise up and bubble forth!

Fill your head and heart with God's Word! Here's a good portion of Scripture to get you started. I have taken the liberty of personalizing it for you. **Please read it out loud.** There is tremendous power as we speak the Word of God!

*"May He grant **me** out of the rich treasury of His glory to be strengthened and reinforced with mighty power in the inner man by the Holy Spirit Himself — indwelling **my** innermost being and personality.*

*"May Christ through **my** faith actually dwell —settle down, abide, make His permanent home —in **my** heart! May **I** be rooted deep in love and founded securely on love,*

*"That **I** may have the power and be strong to apprehend and grasp with all the saints (God's devoted people, the experience of that love) what is the breadth and length and height of it;*

*That **I** may really come to know — practically, through experience for **myself**— the love of Christ which far surpasses mere knowledge without experience; that **I** may be filled through all **my** being unto all the fullness of God — that is, may have the richest measure of the divine Presence, and become a body wholly filled and flooded with God Himself!*

*"Now to Him Who, by (in consequence of) the action of His power that is at work within **me**, is able to carry out His purpose and do **superabundantly, far over and above all that I dare ask or think — infinitely beyond my highest prayers, desires, thoughts, hopes or dreams —***

"To Him be glory in the church and in Christ throughout all generations, for ever and ever. Amen — so be it" (Eph. 3:16-20, The Amplified Bible).

Conclusion

"Thus says the Lord, the God of Israel: Write in a book all the words that I have spoken to you" (Jer. 30:2, Revised Standard Version).

I sincerely hope that this book has been a source of blessing to you.

I pray that you now feel challenged and motivated in the area of Children's Ministry. PLEASE, PLEASE don't just be concerned about running a good program and keeping the children "entertained" during the sermon.

Be concerned about your ministry to families. Be concerned about seeing children — sensitive and obedient to the Holy Spirit — rising up as confident, vital, ministering little members of your local church; a generation of children who **know their God** and do great exploits for Him in the midst of the darkness of this present world!

May Jesus bless and guide your steps as you strive to be a disciple who brings the little ones to Him.

I invite you to join with me in praying that the Lord will move in a sovereign way upon the hearts of the children; that He will raise up a mighty army of SOLDIERS WITH LITTLE FEET!

Hugga-Wugga (Dian Layton)

HUGGA WUGGA S
Kingdom Curriculum Series

If you just read *Soldiers With Little Feet*, then you already know what you can expect from Dian Layton s materials. The Kingdom Curriculum Series is not just another cute curriculum. It is POWERFUL! Every lesson, every story, and every song is based upon Kingdom principles and is designed to lead your children into a dynamic relationship with the King Himself, Jesus Christ. Children who experience these materials will have a real understanding of who they are as citizens of the Kingdom. They will know what it really means to be saved and filled with the Holy Spirit. They will learn to walk fearlessly with their Lord, praying and believing that King Jesus will answer their prayers. They will learn the power of holy living, humbly listening, and ministering in the anointing of God. And, in the process, they will learn Bible stories from some very unique perspectives and dozens of memory verses, Hugga-Wugga style! Dian s refreshing approach brings LIFE, both to the children and to those who teach them....

To view Dian s KINGDOM CURRICULUM and other
materials, visit the MercyPlace website
at **www.destinyimage.com**.

Dian prayerfully considers each request she receives to minister at churches, conferences, camps, and retreats. She travels under the umbrella of MercyPlace Ministries, the home of Family Revival Weekends. To find out more about this dynamic ministry to families, please visit the website or contact Dian at:

Destiny Image
P.O. Box 310
Shippensburg, PA 17257
e-mail: dml@destinyimage.com

Printed in the United States
44865LVS00001B/7-45